# Happiness *is* an Option

**Thriving**
(Instead of
Surviving)
in the Era of
the Internet

## DR. LYNDA M. ULRICH

# HAPPINESS IS AN OPTION

Transcendent Publishing
P.O. Box 66202
St. Pete Beach, FL 33736
www.trancendentpublishing.com

ISBN: 978-1-7353738-1-2

*Disclaimer: The events in this book are memories from the author's perspective. Certain names have been changed to protect the identities of those involved.*

Printed in the United States of America.

# DEDICATION

This book is dedicated to my life-long partner, Dr. Chuck Verderber.

Since the age of fourteen you have made every good idea I had seem possible and all the bad ones seem valuable.

With you, Chuck, 1+1=3.

You are the one who made me appreciate two unique kinds of people in this world: the people who are "multipliers" for the goodness in others and the people I call "the joyful ones."

You, my timeless friend, are a joyful, multiplier of goodness.

# CONTENTS

# ACKNOWLEDGMENTS

People succeed in groups. The insights in this book come from the grace and wisdom that so many people have shared with me since the inception of Ever Widening Circles.

Seven years ago, when I set out to change the negative dialogue about our times, I found myself "a stranger in a strange land." It was only by the grace of so many guides in the digital publishing world that we have survived and are ready for these trying times in which our insights are so desperately needed.

There are so many people who have had a chapter in the Ever Widening Circles story that by now the effort feels like a community project. Most of them were kinder than they needed to be, *right* when I needed them. To all of them, my deepest gratitude.

As for the writing of this book, I have to start with Liesl, my oldest child and COO of Ever Widening Circles. Liesl has done a remarkable job of walking the tightrope between the role of a daughter and the instincts of a global citizen and savvy social innovator/businessperson.

I could not have pulled this together in a way that speaks to all generations without the insights from our Editor-in-Chief, Samantha Burns, whose perspective improves my way of thinking almost every day, and our social media guru, Renee Laroche-Rheaume, whose beaming spirit is a constant reminder of the best that humanity has to bring to our shared journey.

Thank you also to Brittany Nugent and Callie Burkey, who joined the Ever Widening Circles (EWC) team just in the nick of time. Without their constant editing efforts, we would never have been able to bring this book to the public dialogue in ten short weeks. Together, you were the engine that kept things moving forward.

Fundamentally, this book's insights rest on the encouragement of individuals who visit the website often and have generously shared with me why Ever Widening Circles matters, and why we have to keep going. I think of you often.

Stay curious, open, and optimistic. Change is coming.

# AUTHOR'S NOTE

This is a very different introduction from the one I intended to write.

I had intended to open this book from the vantage point of having come through the toughest part of the pandemic, a point where at least some of the panic had passed and we could start to reopen and rebuild with an eye toward a "new normal." Of late that phrase has been bandied about to the point of becoming a cliché, though people probably define it in a number of different ways. In my opinion, the words "new normal" could be equated with "brighter future," one that would include, in large part, a shift in the way we use and experience everything connected to the internet: social media, information, entertainment, and the 24-hour news cycle.

Instead, as I sit here with hands poised over the keyboard, the pandemic rages and our country finds itself in the midst of another upheaval, one that has exposed some of its deepest wounds and one of our deepest sources of division.

The arc of time needs to quickly bend in the favor of honoring what we all have in common.

Ultimately, it is this notion that reminded me why I wrote this book in the first place: so that we can come together, and end the internet chaos that has largely driven the division, rancor, and negativity of the past two decades.

It reminded me of my belief that something like the pandemic almost had to happen so that we might all see that our lives are now intricately and critically connected. We must figure out how to live with our neighbors, regardless of age, culture, and political views, and change our contempt to curiosity. Most importantly, we can take inspiration from the fact that many of the most important leaps in human history have happened just when we thought all hope was lost.

After we identify the losses from great periods of upheaval, it's time to start looking for the *possibilities*. This is the kind of thinking that has brought us through 40,000 years of surviving the elements, scarcity, wars, pandemics, natural disasters, and other events that might have done us in had we not summoned our innate goodness and rallied around conscious bridge-builders who showed us the way forward.

Through most of human history, we did not have the luxury to live in a constant state of division. We needed each other to succeed. Through most of human history, we did not have the luxury of wasting time by complaining or being in a state of gloom about external things that limited us.

Our survival depended on our ability to keep focusing on what we *can* do, not what we can't. And that's the kind of thinking that will bring us out of the crises we are now experiencing, and into a new era.

Yes, it is time to usher in a new era. We all know the one we have passed through in the last twenty years was not sustainable. The division and outrage that still grip our society (seemingly more every day) need to yield to something that has served us since humans walked the earth: discovery.

We need to rediscover all we have in common and recognize how our differences can actually serve us in reinventing the future. That's how most of the important leaps in human progress have come about – an enormous upheaval brought everyone to their knees and forced a kind of collaboration that changed what was possible.

In the pages that follow I'm going to show you how to connect with the world's best-kept secret: a huge wave of progress well underway in the world even now. The key to that is understanding how the internet, social media, and a twenty-four-hour news cycle have evolved and how they are only showing us a (negative) slice of reality. More importantly, we must realize how much power we each have to influence what comes next in that space.

In the process of exercising that power, we will change what we see on the screens in our lives and, ultimately, our worldview. We will see the current limitations in the stories we are telling ourselves about each other and the world around us, and how with four simple shifts we can change those stories by changing the way we interact with the web.

It is still an amazing world, and my goal is to bring you peace of mind and confidence in your future and everyone else's. I will teach you how to find and share evidence of the good and the progress that is taking place each and every day. I also will teach you how to see yourselves, not as the victims of all this chaos, but as the *solution*.

Happiness is an option. We can thrive (instead of just survive) in the era of the internet, if we know a few of its secrets.

– Dr. Lynda M. Ulrich

# CHAPTER ONE

# All that We Have in Common

Kindness, curiosity, and butter.

If there are three things that have made life worth living through the hardest stretches of the last 10,000 years of human history,[1] kindness, curiosity, and butter would have to be considered good contenders in almost every culture in the world.

And recently, those three elements came together to make me think we are ready for another leap in this human experiment.

One lovely Vermont evening about a month into the COVID-19 quarantine, our newly expanded household was sitting around a firepit. We were all still a bit shell-shocked by what had happened to our lives: a once-thriving, thirty-year-old family business had been shuttered; two summer internships in Poland were off; two college graduations were cancelled; and an already isolating Ph.D. program had gotten even more lonely. Our home, which had felt quite spacious when it was just me and my husband Chuck, now seemed much less so with our three kids and their significant others living there.

And as we chatted about the nice evening and poked at the fire, a car unexpectedly drove up the driveway.

It was a very kind friend/co-worker, Samantha, dropping off two beautifully wrapped sticks of butter she had made with wild garlic from her father's farm, not far from where we were all hunkered down. During the lockdown she'd had the time to start getting curious about the edible plants that could be foraged right in her own backyard. Then she had spent a brilliant Sunday morning incorporating the ramps (a kind of wild leek) she'd found into some lovely butter, and thinking of all the people close to her that might appreciate her discovery.

Our whole household went wild over this new arrival to the food scene. You would have thought we won the lottery!

For days we used the butter on various things: eggs, steak, popcorn, and even in a kind of savory oatmeal! The new butter became a multiplier for the gratitude we were starting to feel for life's simple pleasures during this time of upheaval.

And Samantha, the butter-maker? Well, she became a new hero in our lives – one of many creating the momentum for that new era I believe is upon us.

Many of us have been transformed by the pause that COVID-19 forced in our lives, and we've started celebrating the small, ordinary wonders again.

It has given us the chance to get off the treadmills we were on with work and family, and we've found we like the new view of a world with less urgency. We've had time to let our minds wander and time to do a little something nice for someone else. Some of us did a lot of worrying in the beginning, but as we realized our worrying couldn't change anything we found peace in just doing what we could do.

After just a few months of the pandemic, in many ways a new day had already dawned.

The experience confirmed suspicions I'd had for a few years: namely, that a change was in the air and a new era was beginning. It was just, for the moment, out of sight.

What if right when COVID-19 hit, we were at an emotional tipping point in our tolerance for the divisive, negative noise in social media, the internet and the 24-hour news cycle?

What if the global pause was like someone pulling the cord on the emergency brakes?

This could be our chance to begin again.

I believe we are about to witness one of the most important leaps in human progress: we are going to get on with the business of progressing to a better future for us all.

Expectations have already shifted. Have you noticed that the upheaval of COVID-19 has left many of us expecting others to be more patient, thoughtful, light-hearted, and flexible?

We have started celebrating the "givers" and the "doers" – the tireless good people in essential services; neighbors doing what they can for each other; businesses finding ingenious ways to carry on and serve their communities. In fact, the people who were getting the shares on social media in the early days of the quarantine were those who had stopped complaining and started solving common problems in clever, often funny ways.

The scope and weight of all this upheaval may have finally tipped the balance in favor of empathy and understanding.

# I suspect we are going to see that *goodness* can be viral too!

We have a new awareness of all we have in common.

When this all started, ordinary people suddenly had to educate their own kids at home and navigate the grocery store as if it were a war zone. We had to try cutting our own hair, and we hoped we didn't get a toothache while our dentist's office was closed. And when we were standing in line at the post office or pharmacy with masked strangers, we shared knowing glances that spoke volumes.

We noticed that many of the powerful people in society, the influencers and officials, were experiencing some of the same struggles. The transition was almost overnight and we worked it all out together. In the first six weeks, almost everyone felt the responsibility to act with the interest of others at the forefront.

We also started going on long walks or cooking new things, and we could take a break from remote work to sit outside on a sunny Tuesday morning at 10 a.m. and it felt a bit magical. The gift of a homemade birthday card, loaf of bread, or stick of butter became precious.

Suddenly, gratitude became a normal part of almost every media broadcast as reporters spoke of the heroism and selflessness of the doctors, nurses, and other essential workers on the front lines. "Ordinary," humble doers and thoughtful people also began to win our hearts and attention for the random acts of kindness they might not have had time to perform before.

Most importantly, we started to see how much we all have in common. If you were thrust into the remote-working world, you suddenly began seeing other people's kitchens and spare bedrooms, and they looked a lot like yours!

Even executives were not safe from their children walking into their Zoom business meetings, dangling toys on coat hangers in front of their faces. My personal favorites were the four-year-olds whose heads slowly crept into the video screen from below the desk, wide-eyed and beaming smiles.

Everyone laughed empathetically and an embarrassing moment was transformed into one that was humanizing and unifying. So many of our struggles seemed so much the same.

For a host of reasons, *what we have in common* began to seem so much more important than our differences.

By the second month of the quarantine we started to see men with very bad haircuts sporting baseball caps in the business and entertainment settings. After a few minutes, they almost all came clean and showed us their hilarious misadventures with the scissors.

Cats and dogs, as if sensing a change in the rules, also wandered into these remote meetings, and we noticed that others talk to their pets just like we do! (In fact, I'm now completely comfortable talking to *other* people's pets in the middle of business meetings.) And that's to say nothing of the hilarious no-pants and open-mic mishaps that took place in online classrooms and meetings around the world.

I believe we are getting our sense of humor back about life's imperfections, and that changes everything too.

# With a healthier attitude about these imperfections, issues that once divided us are starting to look like mere details rather than chasms.

Have you noticed the critics who work to shame the other side, the complainers and *chaos-builders* are starting to look out-of-touch and unhelpful?

A fundamental shift began happening in the earliest part of the pandemic.

For quite some time, everyone I spoke to seemed to be in a kind of limbo about where their priorities ought to be, and more and more people seemed to be taking a quiet, personal stand against the division and *chaos-builders* in the world. Many told me they were tuning out the zealots on social media, completely turning off the negative news, and instead were doubling down on what they could do to make the world a better place, right in their own circles.

Yes, just months into the pandemic, the loudest voices seemed determined to stay in division mode, but many of us had moved on.

How about you? Have you sworn at the screens of your TV, computer and smartphone when all the division seemed unhinged and then vowed to tune out the madness? Have you started celebrating small wonders, prioritizing differently and wondering if there is a gift for you hidden in the challenge of this chapter in history?

There *is* such a gift for each of us, and we each have all we need to usher in a new era.

How do I know?

On March 15, 2014, I founded a website called Ever Widening Circles that has since published over a thousand articles about insight and innovation going uncelebrated in the mainstream media. And with great regularity, I speak to thought leaders around the world who are committed to efforts of great promise for the future. We need their insights now more than ever.

They could be pointing us to all that is possible in a brighter future, if we only knew they existed.

These thought leaders have a recipe, which I will share with you in Chapter 12, that each of us can easily apply in our own lives. Best of all, it's one that we can follow to reach our full potential as communities around the world, bringing out the best in our families, friends, neighbors, and co-workers.

## We can change the negative dialogue about our times, and this is the perfect time to rewrite the story about each other, all we have in common, and what's possible in the future.

In the pages that follow, I will share some insights with you about what to do next: how to start seeing and connecting to an enormous wave of goodness and progress well underway in the world that almost no one knows about.

We're calling that wave a *Conspiracy of Goodness* ™ because so many are beginning to propagate this wave without even realizing it, creating a quiet movement that is rescuing our shared future. Once you know how to make a few simple shifts, you will see goodness and progress popping up everywhere.

# CHAPTER TWO

# A Conspiracy of Goodness

You know the feeling you get, once in a while, when you see something on social media so delightful that you just have to share it?

You don't stop to think about how it will make you look or which friends you will alienate because it seems so inherently full of wonder that you know it will touch everyone it lands on. Then you look and find it's had 9,876,330 likes.

I believe that in those instances we are recognizing we share a common compass for goodness. Some things strike us as true north at our common core, no matter our age, culture, or politics. In this day and age, this is where we need to be working from.

Look at all the most wildly successful, generous movements and you'll find an element of compassion there that unites us. Think about things as diverse in impact and historical significance as the Underground Railroad[2] of 1831 and the ALS Ice Bucket Challenge[3] of 2014, or the way the American Revolution captured people's dreams of possibility. Even the Harry Potter series, while fictional, created a global cult following around the idea that children might possess the power, and the magic, to change the future for the better, for everyone.

In all those examples, large and small, and many more I could give you, people followed a compass for compassion that they shared with others, even if they had little else in common.

If you took the icy challenge, read every Harry Potter book twice, have ever donated to food banks, adopted a rescue animal, recycled meticulously, helped out during the pandemic or with some sort of disaster relief effort, you are following that compass for compassion.

Is it a coincidence that the words *compassion* and *compass* have so much in common?

Throughout this book I will refer to the *Conspiracy of Goodness* I see taking place in the world. I originally heard the phrase from a thought leader, Brian Kriftcher, who, upon hearing about the work I do, was reminded of a story his father used to tell. It is the perfect example of what we can do together when we follow that common inner compass.

> Not many people know that during World War II, the small village of Le Chambon, France saved 3,500 Jews from the Nazi concentration camps. Without any formal organization and at great risk to their own lives, the villagers managed to hide thousands of strangers (many of them orphaned children) for several years.
>
> In 1987, Rabbi Harold M. Schulwies was giving a talk in Europe about this chapter of WWII, which he called *The Conspiracy of Evil*. At the end of his talk, an old man stood up to say that he had been one of the Dutch rescuers who had hidden a Jewish family.
>
> "Why does everyone focus on the conspiracy of *evil* that was WWII?" the old man asked. "Do you think I could have hidden an entire Jewish family in my home without the active

cooperation of the mailman, the milkman, and the neighbors? No, for every one person saved, there were seven who were 'rescuers.'

There was," he said, "a conspiracy of goodness."[4]

Nice, huh?

When I first read that story, I was rooted to the ground. All the signs of goodness and progress I'd seen in my work with Ever Widening Circles over the past few years came flooding back – all the thought leaders I'd spoken to, all the hours that the Ever Widening Circles team had spent pitching article ideas at each other.

Suddenly, it was as if all the pieces of a great puzzle were beginning to fit together, and they were revealing a new picture of the future.

I believe the story of Le Chambon is but one example of a process that has served us throughout human history, that a *Conspiracy of Goodness* is a pattern which has repeated itself over and over.

This is the way social change happens – almost imperceptibly at first, when one by one we start quietly turning away from the prevailing trend because it offends us somewhere at our core. Does that explain your feeling of overwhelm and disgust when you spent your lunch break scrolling through hundreds of mediocre, meaningless, or just plain mean pieces of internet content?

Think about it for a minute – humans have a habit of adopting really primitive practices that eventually collapse under the weight of the chaos they create. We then leap forward in our way of thinking, and a new era opens. Are we there now, on several fronts?

History is brimming with examples. Take the practice of gladiators fighting each other to the death in the Colosseum as the crowds cheered on. That made total sense in the year 50 AD,[5] and then eventually it didn't.

And what about the massacre of Jews and Muslims during the Crusades, or the colonization of countries and oppression of their native populations? We now gasp at the fact that those practices were acceptable. Slavery made sense to many people throughout history, as did child labor at the start of the Industrial Revolution. So did segregation, apartheid, and denying women the right to vote!

All those things made perfect sense to many — until one day, they didn't.

Here's what my instincts tell me: all those merciless practices eventually became so at odds with what makes us human – compassion, kindness, and our reverence for beauty – that ordinary individuals quietly started taking steps *away* from them. They were following the common compass for compassion.

In Le Chambon, and all the other historical circumstances I just mentioned, person after person did what they could to balance their actions and beliefs with their *humanity*. Together, they formed a quiet but powerful Conspiracy of Goodness that, like a rising tide, eventually reached a tipping point that changed society's way of thinking, creating a new normal that lifted more people up.

Perhaps the way you and I are privately taking actions against the overwhelming negativity is at the heart of a "conspiracy" for our times. Are we conspiring against the chaos-building, quietly taking matters into our own hands when it comes to making the world a better place?

The answer is yes, what we are doing qualifies as a *positive conspiracy*. As it turns out, the word "conspiracy" is derived from the Latin word *conspirare,* which means "to agree." If you break *conspirare* down you get "con," meaning "together," and "spirare," which means "to breathe."

"Breathe together" seems to be a delightful way to describe what people are quietly doing when they decide to be kinder than they need to be in their daily lives. This chapter in history has brought some of those impulses to the surface. Instead of holding their breath and waiting for someone else to come along and make a difference, it seems that many have informally agreed to do what they can to breathe life into a better shared future.

Ordinary people like you and I are doing brilliant, quiet things, just like the milkman, the mailman and the neighbors in Le Chambon, France did—and I believe we are breathing life into a new era together. At the core of that era will be kindness and curiosity (and, if we are lucky, butter may be there too!).

# CHAPTER THREE

## Be Kinder Than You Need to Be

"Be kinder than you need to be." That's what I whispered to my husband at the beginning of a long flight back from South Africa, when a young couple settled in behind us with a screaming eighteen-month-old baby.

It was after midnight Johannesburg time, and everyone boarding the plane was exhausted by a long delay. Writhing in protest on her powerless father's lap, the baby was just old enough to plant both feet in a resounding kick to the back of my seat and send my water flying. It was going to be a long flight.

So we did the only thing we could do: settled into having a sense of humor about the situation. And, as the kicking and screaming escalated, we even fell into one of those moments when we couldn't stop giggling.

We then saw what happens when we react less and pause to think about our options more. The young mother of the baby in meltdown got up from her seat and with a warm, grateful smile started handing out professional-grade earplugs and chocolate candy kisses to every passenger within ten seats in all directions.

Every single person she leaned into with her apology and gratitude went from stiffened and irritated to relaxed and compassionate. After that, the whole section of the plane had an awkward giggle with her, and I'm sure most of us were thinking about how we had been there once ourselves. The moment had revealed how kindness and comp-assion can connect us all almost instantaneously.

# In this new era that we are sharing/ experiencing, I believe it's going to be all about *what we have in common.*

Chuck and I understood their pain. We'd been taking our kids *everywhere* since kindergarten. By the age of eighteen, they had slept on plywood in Tibet, run around in the IRA headquarters in Northern Ireland, and seen some harsh realities in the Kalahari Desert.

They have stayed in hotel rooms where you don't want to take off your shoes before going to bed. They had been in one of the most dangerous slums in the world and almost slept under the car with us when we got lost in the Andes Mountains one night.

*A lovely late afternoon in Northern Ireland.*
*The crew still smiling after we climbed that mountain behind us.*

And through it all, they were hilariously good sports because both my husband and I come from hardworking people who would go to extremes to help a stranger and just take life as it comes.

There's a good chance you had at least one caring adult like that when you were growing up. That's exactly why the current era—with its divisiveness and so much fear—has felt so wrong to most of us. Through our impressionable years (remember those?), we saw lots of people with extraordinary capacity for turning the other cheek and who met disappointment with remarkable grace. They were the ones who in an earlier time kept the Conspiracy of Goodness humming like an engine despite whatever cards they were dealt.

# *Being kinder than you need to be* is how my husband and I both learned to respond to the harshness of the world.

Chuck and I both needed to grow up fast. We met at age 14; found a way to navigate our own individual childhood tragedies; were made to take on a lot of responsibility early in our lives, and were schooled by mentors and family who put kindness before self-interest at every major crossroad.

He grew up in a huge, loving family beside the railroad tracks. His father laid tile for a living and his mother found ways to stretch the grocery money for seven children, one with cerebral palsy and another who needed to spend a summer in a body cast. On Saturday mornings Chuck would collect the money from his newspaper route and then hide out in a nearby junkyard with a dozen donuts and a gallon of milk, all to himself! It was a complex and joyful upbringing.

My parents had survived disastrous childhoods with remarkable coping skills. At age eleven, my mom had crossed the entire United States alone after being orphaned. She went on to become a nurse. When he was fifteen, my dad had been forced from his home by a tyrannical father. Through sheer force of will, he became one of the last of the family doctors who delivered your baby, took out your appendix, and put your kid back together in the emergency room after a motorcycle accident. You had his home phone number and he made house calls.

He taught me the value of empathy.

The foundations for this book lie in the way my parents made their way from absolutely nothing to lives of constant learning, service to others, and trusting the world around them.

At a time when all that most people saw of the wider world were news clips from the Vietnam War, every horizontal surface in our home was covered with National Geographic magazines. My parents leaned on them for evidence that the wider world was nothing to fear.

Things were far from perfect in the homes Chuck and I grew up in, but they seemed to find that sweet spot for children to learn from unsupervised adventures.

Our little farming town of Lincoln, Illinois sat in the middle of endless, flat expanses of corn and soybean fields that stretched to every horizon. That one-dimensional world invited us to look at every summer day like a giant game of *Chutes and Ladders*. I'm so thankful that my childhood memories are filled with things like building dangerously high tree houses all on our own, riding bicycles like the wind on unfinished stretches of highway, and playing countless hours of backyard sports without the constant minding of adults. The only reality check we had was that we had to be home by the time the porch or streetlights came on.

*Chuck and Lynda, age 17, at their high school prom.*

On our family farm, I learned to drive a backhoe, weld, slaughter hogs, grow vast gardens, and buck eighty-pound bales of hay, all out of necessity. I was allowed to raise orphaned raccoons in my bedroom, ride dangerously wild horses to far-off hamlets, and wear elaborate jewelry to school that I had made from colorful bottle caps. I was an artist from the first time a dab of finger paint touched paper, and by my early teens I was being paid to paint humorous murals in hospitals and rewarded for extravagant science fair projects that involved both art and science.

But the real adventures started when Chuck began to dribble and shoot a basketball better than most young players in the country. He became one of the twenty McDonald's High School All-Americans and was recruited by the University of Kentucky the year they won the NCAA championship and were, arguably, the premier basketball program in the world. There he played against people like Michael Jordan, James Worthy, and Isiah Thomas, and he was eventually one of the only people at Kentucky to have been chosen as team captain for two years.

Sounds idyllic, and it was a wonderful ride in many ways, but the realities of the bigger, crueler world were apparent from day one, and luckily we faced them together. We were suddenly forced to find a place for intense pressure, money, and fame within our understanding of *kindness*.

The 1980s was a transition era for both college and professional basketball. The flood of interest and money in both had created fertile ground for the excesses like drugs, fast women, and hundred-dollar handshakes. It was a lot to process for two kids who had grown up weeding soybean fields.

And then there were the many people who arrived on the scene to expand our notions about what it means to be *kinder than they needed to be.*

Chuck had gone off to college with a cardboard suitcase, hand-me-down shoes from a local beekeeper (he was the only other giant person in town and his shoes were very stylish...not!), and the seventy-five dollars he got for graduation.

# And right off we learned that one of the greatest kindnesses you can offer someone is to help to protect their dignity.

There were many people who made sure Chuck could survive the limelight with his pride intact. One family made sure he had a suit and tie to wear to important banquets that started almost immediately. Another coached him on how to give a decent talk when he had public speaking engagements, and yet another covered how he should talk to journalists. One family taught him the nuances of proper table etiquette so he felt comfortable at elaborate dinners with wealthy basketball backers from Lexington, Kentucky's extravagant horse racing industry. Then there was the family who offered him a place to crash, where he could be himself, as vulnerable as any eighteen-year-old boy. They treated him like one of their own.

Every generous meal and every word of support and caution reinforced our notions that even in the most intense situations, kind people will show up and all we have to do is invite them into our lives.

Being thrust into the big leagues of the sports world so early in life was a crucible for finely tuning the values we'd learned from small town America.

We learned that everyone, no matter how powerful or influential, puts their pants on the same way—and has the same struggles that the rest of us endure. Some of the most happy and successful people we met in the Kentucky years taught us that you must march to the beat of your own drum. I suspect that's what triggered our courage to start making a lifetime full of seemingly counter-intuitive decisions.

In 1982, when Chuck was drafted by the Chicago Bulls in the seventh round, we found ourselves at a fork in the road.

Would we remember our upbringing, or follow the shiny lights?

We didn't even open the envelope containing the Bulls' contract.

We had seen some of what that life might look like and chose instead to roll the dice on a future out in the wider world. Chuck signed a contract with a basketball team in Spain, and that was the beginning of our adventures off the beaten path and all around the globe. After Spain we spent some time living in Italy. We acquired Irish passports and dual citizenship, and ever since have considered ourselves citizens of the wider world.

*This is what laundry day looked like during our "life on the road" phase in Italy. All our worldly possessions were in this photo.*

After dental school, we moved to Italy to practice dentistry and a series of unfortunate events left us living on a budget of $9 a day in campgrounds where we cohabitated with circus performers and other "adventurers" for three months. It was one of the strangest and most wonderful times of our lives.

Eventually we returned to the U.S., both became dentists, and decided to put down roots in Northern Vermont, about an hour south of Montréal, where we've raised our three worldly kids.

Before I move on from the stories of my past that have brought you and I together, there are some quirky odds and ends, specifically four pieces of the "Dr. Lynda story" that gave me the compassion, creativity, optimism, and expansive worldview one would need to set off on a journey to change the negative dialogue about our times.

**My compassion comes from my love and curiosity for nature.**

Ever since I was a child I had been fascinated with wildlife, and I brought that right into the homelife Chuck and I created for our family. For many years, we were the only people in Vermont licensed to raise orphaned moose and large animals for the Vermont Fish and Wildlife Department. We raised and released a dozen orphaned animals every summer: fawns, foxes, porcupines, skunks, raccoons, seagulls, and the list goes on.

*"How it is that animals understand things I do not know. Perhaps there is a language which is not made of words and everything in the world understands it."*

*— Frances Hodgson Burnett*

*The photo above is our daughter Liesl, age four, with an orphaned moose named Clifford that we raised after his mother was hit by a car.*

Our kids grew up thinking everyone had injured wildlife being nursed back to health on the kitchen counter. We found Clifford, the first of three baby moose we raised, a great home at the Milwaukee Zoo where they cared for him so well that he eventually became the oldest living moose in captivity.

Caring for hapless wildlife required constant creativity. It took a dose of ingenuity and imagination to figure out how to make every new arrival thrive, and when they did, it was like watching a mysterious creation unfold before your eyes.

**My eye for creative wonders also comes from my life as an artist and metal sculptor.**

For the last twenty-five years I have been welding gigantic sculptures with scrap metal from local junkyards to create unusual figures of people, animals, and even a life-sized T-Rex skeleton for our front yard. A life-sized stegosaurus in front of our office has become a local landmark.

*"Art is not what you see, but what you make others see."*

*— Degas*

*My daughter, Louisa, age 12, and me standing with the sculpture we had just finished in the front yard of our dental office.*

My daughter Louisa (who I taught to weld at age twelve) and I have a work in progress right now that will be a life-sized Pterodactyl, eighteen feet (six meters) tall, with a thirty-foot (ten-meter) wingspan. Its skeleton now crouches menacingly in our front yard.

**I've had so many experiences that have taught me that almost anything is possible.**

My fearlessness in that zone stems from that same daughter's unusual birth. Louisa's birthday was supposed to be on Halloween (October 31st); instead, she fell out of me on the 4th of July weekend, after just twenty-three weeks and five days' gestation (the average length is forty weeks). She weighed one pound.

At that time, there were no babies born at twenty-two weeks that survived, so Louisa had a narrow escape. She wasn't even considered a "preemie," but a "micro-preemie." Doctors told us there was little to no chance that she would survive without severe disabilities, a grim supposition that seemed to call into question the wisdom or even compassion of trying to save her life.

Yet she did survive, and then we made it through day after day in the intensive care unit. Her diaper – which was too big for her in the photo below – was just a bit bigger than a playing card folded in half!

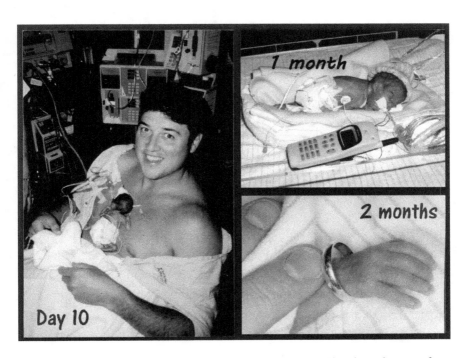

*This photo collage is of her on her father's bare chest, smaller than the size of our cellphone at 1 month old, and at two months, her father's wedding ring could fit on her wrist.*

That first six months was a "boot camp" for dealing with the challenging chatter inside one's head. Living with a child on death's doorstep for many months teaches you to manage your perspectives with the agility of a ninja, and for that reason, Chuck and I tend to look at every rough patch not as a tragedy, but as a problem to be solved.

Miraculously, Louisa not only survived, but grew up to have absolutely no sign of her rocky start. She graduated high school with a provisional patent on an entirely new kind of wind turbine and is convinced that she is here for a reason.

(Yes, her early start is a story all on its own. I've written an article[6] for Ever Widening Circles about that adventure with twelve insights we learned and use every day. *Being kinder than you need to be* is a mantra all over that experience!)

**Lastly, my expansive worldview comes from reading voraciously.**

I believe we each have at least one gift akin to a superpower, and if someone asked me mine I would have to say it's my curiosity. I have an insatiable need to learn more.

Long ago I decided that if I could not investigate everything for myself I would read about it. I will read anything from *The New York Times* bestseller list of business books to books by astronomer/philosopher Carl Sagan, thought leader Malcolm Gladwell, and comedian Zach Anner. My bedside table is stacked with books about the ocean, neuroscience, prehistoric creatures, engineering, philosophy, and biographies of a truly eclectic assortment.

I have the same impulse to learn about everyone I meet; it's what has led to the countless wonderful conversations I've had with thought leaders around the world for Ever Widening Circles.

*"Sometimes it's a form of love just to talk to somebody that you have nothing in common with and still be fascinated by their presence."*

*— David Byrne*

And that brings us back to the very best thing that these experiences have instilled in me: a sense of wonder.

Looking back, Ever Widening Circles seems a logical outgrowth of my life spent finding the gift in almost every disappointment and learning from people who were kinder than they needed to be.

*Dr. Lynda and Dr. Chuck sharing a laugh and a sigh.*

If you give me a solid answer, I'll ask an even better question next!

# CHAPTER FOUR

## It is Still an Amazing World!

In 2013, I was an ordinary web user, which is to say I could hop around the internet to buy a pair of work boots, watch something interesting on YouTube, and post pictures of my kids on Facebook. That all changed one day when I received an email from a nineteen-year-old boy who I had known since he was a toddler.

Cameron was writing to me from a very bleak part of the world where he had landed after signing up for the army, a way he'd thought he could make a positive impact. Instead, what he found there, and the negative news he was getting from home, had left him hopeless.

In the email, he made comments familiar to almost all of us these days. *"Every time I hear the news, I get more depressed." "It's hopeless. Nothing I can do would make any difference." "Every time I look at social media I feel more terrible about my life."*

He had lost confidence in humanity and the future for us all, and yet for some reason he had thought to write to me.

As I read his note, I realized that my impulse to be truly present for people and loving them for all their precious uniqueness had been a good instinct to follow. There was a deeper purpose to the tears, hugs, high fives, and lots of laughter I had shared with patients in my office each day.

Our many years of adventures had taught me that we can't be happy all the time, but in almost every situation, we can find something to be grateful for.[7]

Dr. Chuck and I had spent twenty years in rural Vermont working hard to keep the humanity in healthcare. And no matter what circumstances my patients were currently facing, I always made it a point to find something to celebrate in their lives.

And that's why Cameron knew I would be there for him.

I fired off a comforting response to him but it fell far short of the task. So I spent the next three weeks on a mad search of the web for a trustworthy, uplifting place for news and information for everyone, no matter their culture, generation or politics.

I quickly realized that my challenge in this quest was the "trustworthy" bit. Every time I found a possible winner, I'd discover they had a strong political agenda and/or bombarded their viewers with advertising, or provided no clue as to where they'd gotten their information.

And when I could not find any place for news about real progress in the world – with no politics or ads – I decided to build it. That was the moment Ever Widening Circles was born.

Six years and over a thousand articles later, here's what we've learned:

It is *still* an amazing world!

# And, what we give our attention to in the news and on the internet matters, now more than ever.

We *can* change the negative dialogue about our times and we can bring all the good that's happening to the surface, but we have to start by reimagining the internet as a force for progress in the world. I know that sounds like a stretch right now, but it won't be the first time people have used the power of their collective goodwill to change the course of history.

# All the leaps in human progress seem to happen just when we think all hope is lost.

My journey from ordinary web user to web publisher in six intense years has demonstrated that there is a way we can each enjoy a more balanced view of the world around us and usher in a new era.

# We could thrive, even with the knowledge that the world is full of tragedy and imperfection, if we only knew the rest of the story. Happiness is an option.

In this book, I'm going to share many tips with you, including four simple shifts for taking back your peace of mind in an age that seems bent on crushing it.

The first place to start is the mothership in the Ever Widening Circles space: our website at EverWideningCircles.com. There you'll find countless stories of remarkable new perspectives, ingenious innovations, wonder, and the heroes that have been buried in the chaos of the internet.

Our audience is anyone who wants a break from the relentless negativity, and from the cloud of suspicion that seems to hang over every news story these days. We have no agenda other than to restore trust, change the negative dialogue about our times, and prove that this is still an amazing world.

To this day, and through every word on our site, we hold true to promises I made as a result of conducting that search for Cameron:

1) No politics.

2) No ads or commercial agendas.

3) Meticulously cited and trustworthy sources.

When we made those promises in 2014, we had no idea how hard they would be to keep. It seems every topic can be politicized. Unbiased sources have become increasingly harder to find, and the pressure of finding ways to support Ever Widening Circles without advertising has been enormous.

This leads us to an awkward and unavoidable question: if we have no ads, how does the website pay for itself? Well, first, there is one of my greatest pleasures: public speaking. As a part of my work, I am inspiring people all over the world with in-person and online speaking about all the possibilities that open up when we make some small shifts in the cultures of our businesses, organizations, friend groups, and families.

We have also launched an app that we hope people will use as an antidote to the negative news, internet chaos, and meanness on social media. My suggestion is that you put it on the first page of your phone, and whenever a source of dread gets you down, or whenever you get the "breaking news alert" (always bad), you just tap the icon with the little blue circles and instead dive into a source of wonder about the rest of the story.

## What we see on the internet about each other and the world matters because it affects the stories we are constantly telling ourselves.

## There is a constant dialogue running in our minds. Will it be full of dread or possibility? We can choose.

A more balanced worldview will help you show up in a completely different way for life's challenges, both personally and professionally.

We are also consulting with industries and institutions about how to create cultures that celebrate progress and goodness – for employees and customers – in the new era that is dawning.

All of the endeavors in the Ever Widening Circles orbit are in the service of spreading our message of possibility to as many hearts and minds as possible.

This mindset has done that for us countless times already! We have used it to survive some crushing setbacks, and with the help of some wise advisors who arrived on the scene in the nick of time with almost uncanny serendipity, we just kept going. We did what we could do with what we had.

What we've had for resources is a drop in the bucket compared to the big boys in the media, but we are living proof that good intention, human ingenuity, and perseverance can still count for a lot.

The "we" I am referring to is my daughter Liesl and I. Liesl's been my business partner since she graduated from Harvard in 2016, and not a day goes by that I don't feel blessed to have her by my side.

It's a solid recipe for going with our strengths. The Ever Widening Circles effort has me, with my love of people and knack for knowing what can bring us all together, and Liesl, with her millennial drive, eye for design, and knack for questioning every detail and decision we make.

It's a partnership across the generations that is magical.

Indeed, it was after Liesl joined me that things got serious: we went viral in 2018, and at the time of this writing our traffic has almost tripled. In 2019, our visitors spent a total of 32,011 hours with EWC, which is equal to 1,339 days, or 3.65 years! It's clear that a trustworthy place for insight and positive progress is just the right medicine for our times.

In 2018, Liesl launched EWCed.com[8], a free version of our website for students around the globe. Our vision for EWCed is to curate remarkable videos of wonder and innovation from around the web that inspire students to follow their own unique lines of curiosity and fill the traditional learning process with excitement and discovery.

This part of the Ever Widening Circles journey has reminded us of something that is true for both children and adults:

*"You can't be what you can't see."*

*— Marian Wright Edelman*

I still remember the sinking feeling I had when I read that quote for the first time. It seemed to explain perfectly the downward spiral society seems to be in, especially when you consider the negative way in which the news and internet frames that society. We can't be positive and productive if we see nothing but a frightening world of meanness and disorder.

We're hoping to change that, too!

This seems like a good spot for me to lay the keystone of understanding our relationship to the internet.

# The internet is *not* built to give us a balanced worldview.

# It is organized in a way that brings signs of disorder to the top.

# We can change that significantly, and we can start now.

If you're finding that hard to believe, read on. By the time you reach the end of this book you will see exactly what I mean and how you can use it, both on and off the screens of your life. You will discover that enormous wave of goodness and progress well underway in the world. It is the Conspiracy of Goodness of our times—and we are *all* living proof of it.

# CHAPTER FIVE

# The Attention Economy

Now comes the exciting part where you start to transform how you think about your relationship to the negativity you see everywhere. Before we begin, it might help you to know that before I launched Ever Widening Circles I was just as cynical as anyone could be about mass media. I thought we were all at the mercy of a few global media giants and a fiendish marketing complex.

Over time, however, I've come to realize there is something much simpler and WAY less conspiratorial going on here, and it involves us! My adventure from ordinary web-user to web publisher has taught me that the system bends toward what we give our attention to, and that means we actually have *all* the power.

I know that sounds like another stretch, but over the next four chapters you too will see why this is true and how to use it to discover there is no end to the goodness and possibility in our world.

Here's how the internet works: news outlets, social media platforms, advertisers – and anyone else who is creating content – are all after one thing. And it's *not* our money.

## They want our attention.

# The internet is an "attention economy."

I don't believe there were any evil geniuses rubbing their hands together while plotting to take over the world when the internet was created. I can imagine these brilliant engineers ran into work every day following their passions and asking radical questions about what was possible. I suspect their original impulse was to create a way to connect us all and share information in a remarkably faster way.

Mission accomplished. By the early 1990s, we were all starting to celebrate the wonder of "The Information Age."

And then it blew up.

That's when things went wrong. In 1993, there were only one hundred-thirty websites[9] in existence and by 2003[10] there were forty million! Between 1990 and 2000, the number of people on the internet[11] grew at a pace that would have made any attempt to control the chaos futile.

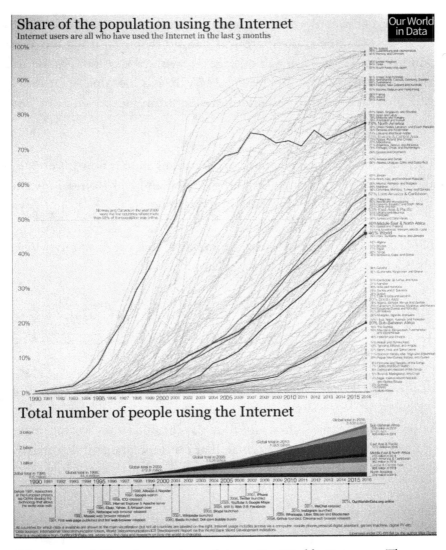

*This is a graph from the amazing website at OurWorldinData.org. There you will find the cold hard data to support my assertion that the world is on a remarkably positive trajectory in many important ways.*

From this chaos emerged a system to govern who found whom. And, like any system, it had a guiding principle, one that assumed *attention* implied *value*. Whoever got the most attention must have information that everyone sees as valuable, right? Sounded good at the time. But as we all know, some content creators had no shame in using our most primitive impulses – fear and outrage – to game the system. With these triggers in place and operating 24/7, it has become increasingly difficult to tell truth from fiction, mastery from inexperience, or news from opinion.

The internet was originally built to connect us all, but now it's dividing us. Our clicks are driving everything – good and bad – on the internet in a frantic game for our attention. Everything.

There is no keeping score of the "good guys" and the "bad guys" when considering content that rises to the top.

## We have an internet that is functioning like a toddler running with scissors. The first thing we need to do is *stop running with it!*

As mentioned earlier, there are four simple shifts that we can make, while using the internet as normal, that can fundamentally change the game the internet is playing with our perspectives.

We can rein this in.

It's important to remember that, given the scope of time, the internet is still in its infancy. A reimagining of its potential is long overdue.

Whenever someone expresses some hopelessness about our being able to change the direction of the internet, I always offer this positive perspective. I tell them I suspect that we are experiencing "growing pains," just as society did during other periods of great change. Take, for example, the level of chaos that reigned in the 1900s surrounding the

Industrial Revolution. Child labor was a tragedy with no end in sight. Twelve-year-old children were forced to work at sewing machines twelve hours a day, and nearly twenty percent of the American workforce was under age sixteen.[12]

Despite many attempts to pass child labor laws, things were dark and horribly out of control throughout the first quarter of the twentieth century. Ironically, it was a catastrophic event – the global economic upheaval of The Great Depression – that paved the road to transformation. The Great Depression led to sweeping reforms in child labor laws in an effort to give those jobs to out-of-work adults.

I've learned that one of the most important questions we can ask ourselves during times of great disappointment is, "How could this be helpful?"

Great upheavals almost always yield leaps in progress. It seems to be how we are wired.

We humans are good at re-imagining what's possible when our backs are to the wall. And I believe we will use the same strengths that have served us for thousands of years – good intention, curiosity, mastery, trustworthiness, creativity, collaboration, and perseverance – to affect a number of long-overdue positive changes now.

What would a world look like where we rewarded those qualities on the internet with our attention?

I will tell you: the people, projects, and businesses utilizing those qualities would rise to the top of the web, the news and social media.

Turns out, we have all the power on the internet. A Conspiracy of Goodness will transform what's happening there too!

# CHAPTER SIX

## PAUSE: Your Click is a Vote

I suspect this opportunity to reimagine our relationship to the internet and negative news could not have come at a better inflection point in our history. I think most of us were ready for a new way forward, no matter our politics, generation or culture.

I haven't heard anyone saying, "Oh, I love all this anger, hysteria, and fear. This is a great time to be alive!"

Nope. No one is saying that.

And I don't hear anyone rooting for more alarm, bickering, and outrage on social media either, though we've probably all been tempted to defend our team or our *sensitive spots*, which of course only adds to the drama.

In fact, I think we all can be excused for letting the chaos of the internet, social media, and 24-hour news cycle wreak havoc with our good nature from time to time. It has become a relentless assault on our character, common sense, and peace of mind.

So how do we get out of this mess?

My journey to become a web publisher has taught me that if we all understood a few fundamental facts, the internet could become a force for good in each of our lives. We would be able to fill our free time there with more joy and wonder than we might ever imagine. On a wider scale, the internet could become a tremendous source of goodness and progress, seemingly overnight.

All we need to do is consider how the internet evolved and understand our personal relationship to the division and chaos there.

Simply put, we are on a feedback loop with the internet that will continue to take us on a downward spiral until we understand how our brains, the negative news, social media, and the chaos on the internet are in an unsustainable relationship.

The bottom line is this:

We humans evolved to optimize our chances of survival. Our brains are hardwired to make signs of disorder and danger the center of our attention, and the internet is built to favor that demand.

It is not built to bring emotions like joy, wonder, peace, hope, love, beauty, gratitude, or kindness to the top of our minds.

You see, there is a part of our brain called the amygdala that has been in charge of our knee-jerk response to the world for hundreds of thousands of years. So long, in fact, that it is often referred to as our "lizard brain."[13]

The lizard brain was our best friend in the Stone Age, and it's what kept us alive in a physically perilous world. It gave us a keen eye for any sign of disorder that might affect our survival.

Here's how those impulses have worked in our favor for 40,000 years:

Imagine that one day you were out picking berries with your Stone Age family. Suddenly, there was a twig snap, and a saber-toothed tiger jumped out, grabbed your sister, and carried her off, never to be seen again. When you told your friends about the day, which part do you think they would remember forever: where you found the good berries, or what the sound of a twig snap meant? The twig snap, of course! It would become a trigger, signaling danger in your mind and the minds of others, forever.

That's how storytelling became a survival mechanism too. And the internet is all about the stories we are telling ourselves, about each other and the world around us.

These days, we don't have to worry about saber-toothed tigers, but that lizard brain is still "on" 24/7, all teed up for survival, ready to reference those stories for context, and make us flee or fight.

And just like that twig snap, those cruel posts we see on social media trigger two impulses in us. We either want to tune it all out (flee) or respond with an angry comment (fight). We forget about all the nice things we saw there too.

We are hardwired to pay special attention to signs of danger and disorder (bad news). In fact, if you are here today, it's because *your* Stone Age ancestors were really good at paying attention to those signs. You and I are here because time and time again, they saved themselves by reacting to danger without a millisecond of thought.

And it's there that the trouble begins with the mass media.

If this very impulsive part of our brain is in the driver's seat when we scroll through social media or are surfing the web, we are effectively on autopilot. And we are going to give our attention – without even realizing it – to signs of disorder: the bad news, the acrimony of social media and clickbait in advertising, without a millisecond of thought!

*"We have met the enemy, and he is us!"*

*– Walt Kelly*

**And now for the good news:**

We have another, more modern part of our brain that can help us out: the cerebral cortex.

This is the area in charge of our *thoughtful* and much more *savvy* responses to the world. It generates more empowering reactions, especially in this digital age when there is so much information and so few saber-toothed tigers.

The cerebral cortex can see a "click bait" headline, photo, or comment on social media and say, *"Hold on a minute! They are just trying to get me to click on that!"*

If we can only pause for a millisecond before we click, we have the ability to put things in perspective and more carefully *decide* what we give our attention to.

So here's the first of four simple shifts that I am recommending for all of us:

# SHIFT #1: PAUSE: Every click you make is a vote,

# because someone is counting every click we make.

# And what we click on, we will get more of.

It's just that simple.

Before I became a web publisher, I think I had a vague idea that this was happening in the background when I clicked around online; but like most of us, I never gave a moment's thought to what that meant. It only became clear to me when we had to start worrying about how many people visited Ever Widening Circles every day. I realized that people's clicks, or lack thereof, were going to determine how much good we could bring to the world.

*A "click" is any way we engage with content, be it clicking our mouse on an image, scrolling through a website, or liking, sharing or commenting on something on Facebook, Instagram, or Twitter.* All of these things indicate that we are giving the content our attention.

All our good will, trustworthiness, and rigorous intention means nothing to the whims of the internet. It is an attention economy.

In fact, we learned quite quickly that the only limit to our ability to reach people with the positive, unbiased content we are committed to creating with Ever Widening Circles was whether we could get peoples' clicks – in other words, their attention!

Who are the "someones" who are counting our clicks?

It is all of us.

It's every person who has ever created anything on the web, from a website or YouTube video to an Instagram or Facebook post. We are all actually counting the clicks we get, aren't we? If something we post on social media gets only one or two likes, we never post anything like that again; or worse yet, we take it down! So you see, we're counting clicks just like major news outlets or big content creators!

It's a bit of a game, actually. Everyone creates something for the internet and then decides what to do next *after* they see if we all click on it. If they get a lot of clicks, they create more content like it.

Remember, it's an *attention economy*. But here's the positive, empowering part…

# We can decide what to give our attention to!

# The fact that someone is counting every click we make can be *a force for good.* It gives us all the power we need to reimagine the role of the internet in our shared future.

I know it sounds a bit crazy because it's so simple, but it's just the way the internet works. If we stopped clicking on things that we do not need more of, a lot would change on the internet!

Isn't it lovely to ponder what the world would look like if we grew into a new way of using the internet? If we just *PAUSED* before we clicked?

## And here's the best news on that front: it doesn't have to be all of us!

The World Economic Forum completed a comprehensive study with the University of London and the University of Pennsylvania. They found that there seems to be a tipping point where a new idea catches on and sweeps through the group. That tipping point seems to be at twenty-five percent.[14] When twenty-five percent of people accept something as the new norm, it can emerge from the shadows of the periphery and sweep through the population like the domino effect.

This means that if just twenty-five percent of us stopped clicking on the craziness – meaning anything that is not making the world a better place for everyone – and started sharing stories of progress, generosity, ingenious collaborations, important new insights and innovation, a new era of goodness and remarkable progress would begin.

Here's a great blog posting that thought leader Seth Godin has allowed me to share:

### Calm Also has a Coefficient[15]

*Panic loves company.*

*And yet calm is our practical, efficient, rational alternative.*

*If you're on a crowded plane and one person is freaking out about turbulence, the panic will eventually peter out. If, on the other hand, six people are freaking out, it's entirely possible that it will spread and overtake the rest of the plane.*

*Panic needs multiple nodes to spread.*

*The same is true with a cabin of 10-year-olds at summer camp. One homesick kid usually comes around and ends up enjoying the summer because being surrounded by others who are okay makes us okay. But three or four homesick kids can change the entire dynamic.*

*While calm is a damping agent, it's not nearly as effective at spreading itself as panic is.*

*The library is usually a quiet place because the dominant cultural narrative in the library is to be quiet. Because it's dominant, the coefficient of its spread is sufficient to keep it that way. We have to expend effort to create environments of calm, because calm has a coefficient that can't compete with panic when it comes to spreading.*

*And Twitter? Twitter has been engineered to maximize panic. Calm is penalized, panic is amplified. And if you are hanging out in real life with people who spend a lot of time on social media and news sites, you've invited all of those people into your circle as well.*

*We can find lots of reasons why fifty years of watching just three dominant TV networks wasn't ideal. But the combination of oligopoly and the FCC meant that none of them spread panic. They weren't built for it. When cable "news" showed up, they discovered that panic was a great way to make a profit. Not to make things better, simply to spread anger and fear.*

*If panic is helpful, of course you should bring it on. But it rarely is.*

*Instead: Curate your incoming.*

*Stay off Twitter.*

*Do the work instead. Whatever needs doing most is better than panic.*

*Being up-to-date on the news is a trap and a scam. Five minutes a day is all you need.*

And that's where my second shift comes into play.

# CHAPTER SEVEN

# IGNORE MORE:
# We Have All the Power

Our work at Ever Widening Circles has us constantly celebrating what will be possible when we reach the point where twenty-five percent of people around the planet realize that someone is counting every click they make. There is just so much useless and unhelpful clickbait that is rising to the top on the internet. But that will all change when we realize our click is a vote, and what we click on we will get more of.

Once we can recognize the game being played with our emotions, a new era will begin.

A key step in that process is our realizing that countless endeavors with the potential to fundamentally improve the future for everyone are not getting our attention because their light is lost in all the chaos and noise. They are working away in obscurity for one simple reason: *We don't know they exist.*

It basically comes down to this:

## The key to reversing what rises to the top for both you and the world is what we ignore!

# We've got to start pausing before we click and ignoring anything that is not helpful and thoughtful.

This is the same basic lesson your mom tried to convey when you came home from school crying because someone called you fat, short, or some other hurtful name. She said, "Oh just ignore them."

I couldn't put it any better! If more of us allow those four simple words to be our mantra while using the internet, we can inspire great change that will eventually ripple out across the globe.

# SHIFT #2: IGNORE the *chaos-builders*.

# We can actually ignore things into obscurity.

# No one is creating content unless people click on it.

# Can't decide who is being unhelpful? Before you click, ask yourself: "*Do we need more of this?*"

Over time, this small shift in what you give your attention to will change what you see on the screens in your world. It will solve a lot of internet-related stress too.

If many of us simply stopped giving our attention to (or stopped clicking on) things we know are not making the world a better place for everyone then mass media would respond very quickly. Because silence (aka no clicks) means the end of most internet endeavors.

So you see, our action, or inaction, could usher in a great moment in history – a time for us to lift our heads up from the treadmills we are on and see that we have the ability to shape our world, not just react to it.

# Every click we make is a vote.

# The choice is ours.

# We can feed the *chaos-builders* or starve them.

You know how everyone frets over the scams, the outrage, and the manipulation on social media? Well, that sort of rampant, unhelpful negativity would have no traction at all if no one clicked on it. Almost any conspiracy we see on the internet would have no traction – no power to hijack the future – if people didn't click on it.

If we all paused to "consider the source" before we shared, liked or commented on the things we see on the internet, social media or the 24-hour news cycle, we would surely realize the power we have to create our own reality.

# If we want a better future for everyone, we simply need to reserve our clicks, our shares, and our comments for the people and places who are making a trustworthy attempt to get us ALL there!

Remember that the *attention economy* of the internet is a house of cards, built on appealing to our worst impulses. Here are two major insights about what we ignore that could change the world:

1) **Stop clicking in "ABC" mode.**

    If you want to stop much of the chaos and noise on the internet from coming your way, I recommend that you stop clicking out of **A**nger, **B**oredom, and random **C**uriosity. What I mean here is the way we mindlessly scroll, scroll, scroll and click in and out of things, stopping only for a millisecond. It's the kind of scrolling and clicking we often do while passing time eating lunch or sitting in a waiting room, et cetera.

    The first thing to realize is that when we are reacting on auto-pilot like that, much of what we click on will be built to trigger our *lizard brain* in some way, creating a steady stream of fight or flight responses and keeping the stress hormones like cortisol far too high for far too long. A steady stream of cortisol means our blood pressure will spike much too frequently, as will our heart rate and blood sugar. This cortisol also impairs the decision-making part of the brain.[16]

    Secondly, if you are scrolling and clicking away in ABC mode, it is just like having voted for hundreds of things that are probably stirring up the chaos we are all suffering with. The volume of that kind of clicking is mind-boggling, and it all counts when it comes to bringing us the internet we see today!

    And *that's* why we are not learning about anti-poaching activist Damien Mander (more about him later in the book) and others who have the key to changing the future. News of their work will not rise to our awareness or give us hope and a more balanced worldview until we start ignoring more of the other stuff.

# When we click, we are teaching content creators exactly what we want more of!

Here are the specific strategies that will change your worldview:

- Never click out of **_ANGER_** in response to a mean-spirited or outrageous social media post. Never.

    If you do, even once, then you are feeding the very monster that is giving us all so much anxiety.

    I know it's painful to resist calling out something that offends us at our core, but we have to keep our composure. Even if you have the best intentions, and you write the savviest response in the world, you just gave that mean-spirited posting a vote that rewarded the content creator. Your comment, no matter how brilliant or compelling, will probably inspire an additional _15-100 angry responses_ from the team that loved that mean posting in the first place. In other words, you've given that mean posting 15-100 more votes!

    Remember, there are no good guys and bad guys on the internet. It's all the same to the people counting our clicks. Your best intentions are irrelevant, except for the basic fact that you can unknowingly give the negativity more "attention juice" in this attention economy.

    **HERE'S THE SKILL:** Mastering your knee-jerk impulses on social media.

    It will take practice and repetition, but I promise, one

day you will be free from the spell that is cast there.

**HERE'S THE REWARD:** When you never engage the negativity, you will stop seeing it! I never see the crazy posts people tell me are on social media because I have ignored them into obscurity in my own orbit. If a lot of people did the same, the loud angry voices would dim.

- Never click on random things out of **BOREDOM.**

  Casually dropping into almost anything that catches your eye is giving attention juice to all the meaningless "shiny object" chaos of the internet.

  Remember, all that content you drop into, then realize is useless and immediately hop out of, is being purposefully created to appeal to our *lizard brain*. And the creators of that unhelpful content are getting rewarded for attracting our attention! It's a simple feedback loop that could be interrupted overnight if most of us knew this was the game being played with our impulses.

  **HERE'S THE SKILL:** Learn to pause for one second and ignore more. Before clicking, ask yourself, "Do we need more of this?" If the answer is no, then *do not click* or engage with the content in any way.

  **HERE'S THE REWARD:** You will begin seeing an entirely new world. If you are using the internet with more purpose and intention, there is no telling how fast you will feel like you are breaking free from the cycle of negativity.

- Never click out of random *CURIOSITY.*

> "Click bait" is painstakingly teed up to appeal to our fears, and that's why we can't help but click on signs of disorder and craziness. We want to know if that curious thing we are seeing is something we need to worry about.
>
> You know that photo of a huge anaconda snake that looks like it has swallowed a human? Well, I'm as curious about that as you are. It is my lizard brain, compelling me to check it out.
>
> Despite that curiosity, I NEVER let myself click on headlines or photos that trigger my worst instincts: not the blobfish; not the tornado destruction; not the scary article titled, "Death Ship: One of Two to Dock in Florida"; and not any images on social media that use words very obviously meant to ridicule others.
>
> Have you ever heard the expression "Curiosity killed the cat!"? Well, in the internet game the cat is our worldview, and it can easily be killed with an outrageous photo, headline, or a social media post that click bait creators are putting out there.

If you *never* fall for "click bait" – and that gets easier and easier with every passing day – then you can keep an almost uninterrupted positive train of thought going with your clicks!

# When troubles do visit you, you are in exactly the right frame of mind to handle them as your best self!

**HERE'S THE SKILL:** Pay attention to what you are paying attention to.

Make your time on the internet a conscious, purposeful adventure. Are you there to feed an interest in nature, gardening, auto mechanics, parenting, or to compare reviews on a new appliance? Get your fill, then sign off and be present for your friends and family.

When you hop on social media, decide what you want more of — perhaps it's joy, humor, or something new about a topic you love — and don't let your attention get hijacked by the chaos-builders.

**HERE'S THE REWARD:** When you ignore all the chaos that used to get your attention (your clicks), you will stop seeing most of the chaos on the web and have the sense that almost anything is possible.

2) **Understand how algorithms determine our worldviews and relationships.**

You know how you and a friend can search the exact same word on the internet and get served different results? This is because of a tool with good intention: the algorithm. Algorithms are like a shortcut. They were created to help us find what we want quicker. Put simply, the algorithms that create our Google search results, our news feeds, and our social media feeds look at what we clicked on last and then guess what we want to see next.

Unfortunately, when we do a lot of mindless scrolling and random clicking on negativity, we are teaching the algorithms that this is what we want to see.

And it's almost a certainty that we are NOT seeing a huge number of other things that might be WAY more positive!

Worse yet, an unfortunate casualty from this system may be our relationships.

Want to know why your conversation with Uncle Jerry or your twenty-two-year-old niece around the Thanksgiving table was so contentious? It's because everything you EACH clicked on last was so vastly different.

Your notions about the world around you – many of your priorities, expectations, and values – have been shaped by what you've each seen on the internet and, over time, that becomes an echo chamber. The information we click on most of the time confirms our own biases and validates all our opinions. It determines the tone of the conversations we have and the choices we make.

And before we know it, all our ideas about what is true have almost no connection to a *shared* reality. Rather, our worldview is as individual as a fingerprint.

No wonder we can't have a normal conversation with good-natured debate, a sense of humor, and a big dollop of curiosity. We are barely speaking the same languages!

**HERE'S THE SKILL:** Learn to be curious about topics that are just outside your current silo of experience. For example, if you've fallen in love with a particular band, you might do a search on them and the type of music they play. This could lead to research on the way music works in our brains.

Or, if you're a huge Star Wars fan, dive into the NASA website (it is amazing), or the international space station website.

That's the way it used to work when people read the newspaper – we would scan the headlines to decide what to read more in depth. Having to read those little snippets about random things in the headlines regularly led to all kinds of serendipity when we accidentally found new things that interested us.

***This tactic does NOT work on the internet, where many headlines are meant to trigger our lizard brain. My point is that you should always leave room for serendipity in your life when it comes to learning about the wider world.

**HERE'S THE REWARD**: You can get along with and find something in common with almost anyone.

You can rest comfortably, feel a thrill for the future, and handle life's ups and downs because you will start seeing a world full of wonders and people with good intention, good manners, and good ideas. They are out there. The internet is only showing us a slice of reality.

Just PAUSE before your click and ask yourself, "Do we need more of this?"

Ignore almost everything that you can't answer with "Yes."

I've learned that the reflexes to do that fluidly, with little to no thought, come quickly and eventually you barely even have to think about it.

The best part of that equation is that the inspiration is cumulative. This can have an amazing snowball effect on your knowledge and insight, as well as your personal sense of belonging and meaning. With everything you ignore, something else will bubble up to the surface to replace it. Those things could be ingenious and exciting, and wonderful for your peace of mind!

# CHAPTER EIGHT

## SEEK Signs of Goodness and Progress

I cry almost every Monday morning now, but not for the reason you may think.

That's when our team gets together to pitch article ideas to each other, and the concepts we run across are breathtaking. It's actually become a funny little game for my team of smart, compassionate, young innovators to make me cry with joy. It's a hoot.

And those joyous pitch sessions every week confirm everything I'm telling you in this book.

I often daydream about what would be possible if everyone, every day, saw the things we see on our screens at Ever Widening Circles.

So if you remember nothing else from this book, when the internet and the news is dragging you down, remember this:

# What we see on the internet is only a slice of reality.

# It is still an amazing world.

And if you want to have a more complete worldview, you are going to want to practice shift #3.

## SHIFT #3: Seek Signs of Goodness and Progress

Don't just let news come at you randomly anymore. If all we know is what the news or social media decides to tee up for us each day, we are bound to think the world and the future is a dumpster fire.

Instead, prepare for a brighter future by *looking* for signs of progress, and you will walk right into it!

We can't expect to be happy, or have a hopeful worldview, if we only know what comes our way accidentally. Taking the time to know more, making time to seek goodness and progress could be one of the most valuable changes we make as a result of this chapter in history.

My decisions every day are vastly improved by knowing about these stories of new insights and people of all walks solving problems. Just think how an increase in your knowledge about the world and the goodness "out there" would improve the way you handle a personal or professional crisis. You would have a much broader perspective on how big the crisis actually is, as well as many more ideas and choices that might lead you forward in unexpected ways.

Think of the inspiration you would draw from knowing more about the vast group of problem-solvers who are out in the world, successfully transforming what is possible. More importantly, repeated exposure to stories of people who are incredibly generous, brave, or clever will give you a sense of grace in how you react to your neighbors, your extended family, friends, and even the person behind you in the line at the coffee shop.

To be more patient, thoughtful, and helpful, we have to be inspired by what can come of those more measured responses, and the thought leaders solving some of the world's most vexing problems are teachers for us all in that way.

To get you started on that journey, I'll share with you just a few of the thousands of stories we are not hearing about and why they so beautifully point to possibility.

## Oliver Percovich and Skateistan

*The following story out of Afghanistan, which we covered on Ever Widening Circles, is one of my favorite examples of hope and the existence of the Conspiracy of Goodness.*

In 2007 Australian researcher and skateboarder Oliver Percovich arrived in Kabul with a couple of skateboards under his arm and an indomitable spirit. Oliver quickly learned two things: the first was that seventy percent of the population was under the age of twenty-five; the second was that almost no investment was being made in this group as Afghanistan tried to rebuild after decades of war. In fact, there was an enormous group of girls and street children who were going completely uneducated.

Oliver took stock of the problem and the tools at his disposal, then got to work creating a community that combined the sport of skateboarding with a movement to increase education and bridge the many divides in Afghan society. News of "Skateistan" spread like wildfire and before long it was serving thousands of kids with hope, knowledge, and a shot at a better life. In just over ten years, Oliver had similar programs with the same mission up and running in Cambodia and South Africa.

The positivity and inspiration in that one article on the Ever Widening Circles website is worth a thousand articles of doom and gloom that might contain some useful factual information but do not show us a balanced view of the goodness happening in places of great struggle.

Look up Skateistan[17] and watch some of their videos. Look into those children's eyes and imagine your own children, nieces or nephews living in conditions like those Oliver's team is working to improve. Their videos are so uplifting that you can feel the incredible changes that team has already made, changes that will ripple out and uplift the whole society. If you have a beating heart, you will find yourself transported to a new realm of delightful possibility. You may even be moved to joyful tears, just as I am every time I watch them.

This is a truly remarkable example of how we can all be propagating the wave of goodness of our times.

It also shows us how we can use the positive aspects of the internet to progress. They have found a way to make their story feel like *our* story: the story of what's possible when humans get it right.

I've met one of the filmmakers for Skateistan and he told some amazing stories about how transformative this work is. We can help them succeed, but only if we know they exist.

The article on Skateistan is just one that points to that common compass for compassion I mentioned earlier. It is also a perfect example of how the internet can bring us together around the things we agree on – like celebrating a brighter future for children, wherever they are, and people like Oliver who see problems that need a champion and use their unique gifts to create solutions. Remember the story of Le Chambon, France, how there were seven rescuers for every person saved? Well, with efforts large and small, people are becoming the "Seven Rescuers" in the Conspiracy of Goodness of our times!

In other words, we do not have to personally educate the children of Afghanistan or save the rainforests; it is through our support of Oliver and other thought leaders that we become behind-the-scenes ambassadors of good will, just like the milkman, the mailman, and the neighbors in the story.

It's important to remember that the negative news cycle and the internet rarely bring us stories of success and progress from struggling parts of the world, and the people in these areas realize this. This is why that article brought Ever Widening Circles more than *six thousand* Facebook fans from Afghanistan.

Here's another wonderful example of people who are following that common compass, and how the internet can become a multiplier for things that bring us together.

## Mason Jar Garbage Cans

Have you heard of people who have refined their consumer habits so effectively that they can fit a whole year's garbage in one mason jar?[18]

There are many, but two notable names in this zero waste community are Bea Johnson[19] and Lauren Singer.[20] Their journeys went from changing their own lives and waste footprints to teaching the world to change as well. They have all kinds of tips for the rest of us, even if we don't want to go to that extreme. I have to say, since writing our two articles on this way of living, we produce about half as much garbage as we used to in our own home, AND we are saving a lot of money!

Google "zero waste community" and you will see an amazing view of the horizon for all of us. Whenever I consider what can happen when we come together, I think of how fast *this* movement is spreading! It is also doing something that points to progress for our world: it is crossing over from being considered a partisan or "green" issue to one that is getting our shared concerns. It's become a matter of common sense. We can't go on producing the volume of waste we have been. Most people who have ever walked a beach or urban river's edge realize we are fouling our own nests.

Here's my own brush with how this new way of thinking about *wastefulness* is catching on:

Over a recent Christmas vacation, I visited my brother Alex on our family farm in Illinois. A former F-15 fighter pilot, he is a very driven and hard-nosed guy. He drives our gigantic John Deere tractor like a Ferrari, and he is the kind of guy who would have a colonoscopy without anesthesia. When he showed up alone for the procedure, the medical staff said they would have to reschedule because he'd need someone to drive him home after being sedated. Instead, he asked himself *How bad could it be?* and told them to just get on with it!

Suffice it to say, Alex is NOT a tree-hugger.

And yet, one morning, as I was having a cup of coffee with his wife, he began cursing and shouting for me to come into the kitchen to see something. I dutifully jumped up – as we all tend to do in response to folks with a military bent – and found him holding two small light bulbs in one hand and a huge array of plastic packaging in the other.

*He was livid.* Livid that he was forced to add that much plastic waste to the world, just to get two small light bulbs. He shouted, "Look at this! THIS is what's wrong with the world! THIS is why beaches look like garbage dumps!"

And he is absolutely right.

And *that* little story tells me something very important to be hopeful about: change is coming.

My brother is the proverbial *canary in the coal mine* – an early notification system about many environmental issues. Why do I consider him a good barometer? Because he is very smart and very cautious about jumping on bandwagons. His default is common sense, every time. So when guys like Alex start becoming irate over things that violate the basics of long-term thinking, like single-use plastics, then it is game over for those who persist in supporting that problem.

The number and depth of articles we come across about solutions to our world's plastic problem are proof that the wheels are turning. In fact, these solutions are popping up all over the place – just open an incognito window to improve the variety of responses you get from your Google search, and then search "solutions to the plastic problem" and you'll find great examples of the Conspiracy of Goodness wave currently happening in that one niche.

And that same level of energy is going on in many, if not most, aspects of our existence. However, you are unlikely to see these stories rise to the top until we all start pausing and ignoring more.

Now we will study how each of us propagates waves of progress in remarkable ways. Together, we lift all of us up.

# CHAPTER NINE

# SHARE Signs of Hope You Discover

As mentioned earlier, the rationale for the fourth small but critical shift is pretty simple: if we stop giving our attention to the chaos-builders on the internet, the negativity will eventually shrink in volume. But that's just part of it. In order to usher in a new era of goodness and progress, we have to consciously replace that negativity with things that support our ability to create a better shared future.

With the knowledge that every click we make is a vote, we can each be part of making positive content rise to the top.

The power in that effort will be in what we share.

## SHIFT #4: SHARE Signs of Goodness and Progress for all.

## We have the power to bend the *attention economy* of the internet in a positive direction.

## The momentum will come from what we share.

We all know that what we share has the ability to spread wildly through the web. This is as equally true of stories of goodness and progress as it is for those of chaos. The people who create the news and content for the web then move to meet whatever we are giving our attention to.

Remember, by clicking on all the chaos, negativity, fear, and disorder we have been teaching content creators that this is what we want more of. Now we can send a different message. We can PAUSE, IGNORE MORE, and then share the ingenious, the kindness, and the wonder.

We can use that insight to usher in a new era together. We can continually create positive change together on a large scale.

Here is something you may not have considered but is very important to achieving that goal: there is a vast difference between a "like" and a "share."

A like on the internet is a nice little gesture that gets seen by our closest friends. A share, on the other hand, goes out to hundreds, if not thousands, and can start a wave that takes on a life of its own. So when you see that story of the neighborhood kid who raised four hundred dollars for the animal shelter, don't just like it – share it. It *is* remarkable that a ten-year-old would help homeless pups so significantly. He can inspire his peers and everyone else to play/do our own courageous part. These are the things that need sharing, not some political point of view or quick quote. This is how things go viral and add to this wave of progress that I'm pointing you to today!

# The thought leaders who are building a better future for all of us need our clicks and our shares.

Remember, most people who are trying to solve problems, be it bullying or climate change, are toiling away in obscurity in quiet corners of the internet, fighting for every mention in the press they can get.

And because they are not winning the attention game, they do not get the support they need to thrive and become an example of progress for us all.

Success in our current *attention economy* has almost nothing to do with merit.

Here's how it works. Let's say you've found a proven way to save the rainforest using old cell phones. As soon as you put that big idea on the internet, you are competing head-to-head with someone claiming to have a formula for a super-duper male enhancement potion made from the horns of the last rhinos on Earth.

This person uses a clickbait photo or headline that is more attention-grabbing than yours, and he wins. A much larger number of people click on his link while your project remains in obscurity and will eventually disappear.

To make matters worse, in our current system, the male enhancement project gets funded by people who see how much attention it got. Then advertisers and search engines continue to amplify its "success."

That's it.

Currently, if you are trying to sell a product, service, or idea that could change the world for everyone, there is only one playing field. Put simply, great ideas live or die on the vine based *not* on their merit, but on how good they are at getting our attention in the scrum we call the web. The *chaos-builders* are getting all the oxygen on the internet while countless good ideas and thought leaders remain in obscurity.

Countless innovators have ingenious solutions to our most vexing problems; they are just waiting to be "discovered" and celebrated. Only then will they be able to scale up and change the future.

The good news is that in the digital age, we can support them in so many ways, even if we can't do it financially. For example, you can post about their work on social media. You can even reach out to their project coordinator to find out exactly what they need to help get the word out, be it volunteering, lobbying, or legislation, and add that information to your posts. That will do worlds of good for their brand, as well as your own.

So you see, we can be like one of the Seven Rescuers in the Conspiracy of Goodness story!

We don't have to physically go save the rainforests in person, but we can do all sorts of simple things to support the work of innovators who are saving them, and make sure those endeavors rise to the top of the internet. (I'll talk more about Topher White and The Rainforest Connection later on in the book.)

## By celebrating goodness, we can take others on a journey they could not have gone on without us.

Here are two very valuable things you can offer projects that are making the world a better place for everyone.

1)  Give them your attention.

    a)  Share them all over social media regularly.

    b)  Read, engage, and comment on everything they put out: newsletters, special events, letter writing campaigns. (Really get behind them!)

    c)  Contact them to see how you might be able to help.

2)  Donate what you can, even if it's just a few dollars.

    a)  I know how these social innovators operate because I have been one. It is a constant shell game with priorities and deciding where to put the next nickel so that progress can be made. Social innovators will wildly appreciate every act of generosity that comes their way. They also have an uncanny sense for value; they know where our money is best spent to make an impact. We can all feel good about that.

At Ever Widening Circles, we do our part by giving innovators a place to be heard, and you the opportunity to like and share their stories, thus becoming part of the Conspiracy of Goodness. From these stories, we have also seen a recipe for success in the new era emerge (more on that in Chapter 12).

Thinking about that bright future always brings to my mind a story about Carl Sagan, the famous astronomer-physicist of the 1970s, 80s and 90s. Sagan was one of the early great communicators who popularized the wonder of science by speaking to all of us in a common language that was somehow close to our core.

People used to ask him if he thought man would ever be able to travel to Mars. He thought a better question was, "Who will we need to *become* to be able to get to Mars?"

Was he suggesting that it might be time to start leading with the newer, more thoughtful part of our brain? What if humans are just about to make another leap, and the unhelpful state of mayhem on the internet is the catalyst we need to get to it?

Can we evolve into our better nature? This, I believe, will all depend on our learning to control what we give our attention to.

Here's one of my favorite stories about the kind of insight and innovation that will be rising to the top of our awareness when more of us start sharing goodness and ignoring the chaos-builders.

In July of 2019, an event occurred that was so remarkable and positive that it could have been a cause for a global celebration of *what's right with the world*.[21] It might have been a news story that brought us together around a wonder similar to that of looking up at a brilliant, starry night sky. Instead, on the day it occurred, I feel it went rather underappreciated, as so many truly "good news" stories do. Since then I've made it a point to ask people if they knew of this milestone in human history, only to find that most do not.

Did you know that right now, there is an amazing spacecraft making its way through our solar system that needs no fuel – ever? It's called LightSail2[22] and on July 23, 2019 it slowly, flawlessly unfurled a sheet of reflective material forty times thinner than a sheet of paper and the size of a third of an acre. It will use photons of light as its fuel source to gently push its adventures through space.

To give you even greater perspective on this achievement, clever humans have been pondering the possibilities of sailing through the cosmos since the seventeenth century. In 1608 the astronomer Johannes Kepler gazed up at the night sky, watching the bright flash of light that would eventually become known as Halley's Comet. He later wrote about his observation in a letter he penned to Galileo (who you might have heard of!):

*"Provide ships or sails adapted to the heavenly breezes, and there will be some who will brave even that void."*

*— Johannes Kepler*

Indeed, there is something about space travel that strikes us at our core. The possibilities there have been the stuff of our most wondrous imaginings ever since the publication of Jules Verne's 1865 novel *From the Earth to the Moon.* In 1895, H.G. Wells imagined a martian invasion in *The War of the Worlds,* and Alex Raymond's 1934 comic strip *Flash Gordon* became a franchise that continues to this day. In 1966, Gene Roddenberry's *Star Trek* brought space adventures into households all over America and expanded our imagination of what is possible.

Given this rich history, The LightSail2 is certainly the kind of thing that puts the awe in awesome. Maybe that's why this leap for all of mankind was crowdfunded by more than *forty thousand donations* from ordinary people[23] all around the world! (A side note: crowdfunding is a terrific example of how we can all become like the Seven Rescuers from the Conspiracy of Goodness story. We don't have to start the big project, but with a small investment we can help make it possible.)

And just for fun, you might be interested to know that the group that organized this whole LightSail2 endeavor was the Planetary Society,[24] which Carl Sagan founded in 1980. Its current CEO is Bill Nye,[25] who you may know as "the science guy."

The whole story was full of wonders and delightful serendipity, and yet many people have not heard about it. Could that be because we are not clicking on signs of goodness and progress often enough? Could it be because we have not sent a message to news and content creators that what we *really* want is good news?

If you've been reading along you know that the answer to both questions is yes. I believe we do want good news. I also think people would care about the other thousand things we've published articles about on Ever Widening Circles, if only they knew about them.

Remember those famous novels I mentioned above. If we want to read fictional accounts of life in space, doesn't it stand to reason that we'd want to know about the real thing?

# CHAPTER TEN

# Who Will We Become?

The pandemic and upheaval have changed many things about our world, and while the extent of these changes still remain to be seen, one thing is for sure: we have been given the gift, the responsibility, and the very rare chance to begin again.

It's wise to ask ourselves such timely questions as, *Who will we become?* What will we prioritize? Who and what will we give our attention to going forward? What will we believe about each other? How can we more quickly discover what we have in common and use that in wonderful ways?

## It's a good time to put some thought into what we are *discovering*.

## If we've discovered one thing from this chapter in history, it's that we are all connected.

If we thought we could still operate as "islands" – as isolated individuals, families, communities, states or nations – that notion has been completely shattered. We now know that every human being on our planet is irreversibly and fundamentally connected on many levels, in some ways that are knowable and others that are invisible. No amount of isolation, hand sanitizer, or media messaging can change what we experienced as we saw the coronavirus make its way around the world.

What if we used that shared experience to remind us of all we have in common?

I believe that's the crucible, where a wonderful, shared future will be forged out of the wreckage of our experiences, marking the end to this era of division.

The innovators have taught me to ask myself two questions in times of great disappointment:

## What good could come of this?

## How could this be helpful?

As disheartening as all the arguing in society has been, I suspect our shared experience and our diverse points of view might hold a silver lining for us if we can rise above the turmoil and look at our situation sitting shoulder to shoulder.

I believe we have been moving from an "I" world to a "we" world for quite some time, but the transition is now happening faster than ever. And here's the beauty in that: if we can pause and shift what we give our attention to, we can combine our differences to come up with ingenious ways to solve problems. The potential is all wrapped up in our ability to pause and shift to a more thoughtful mindset.

It can be done. I've been studying innovative problem-solvers for many years now, and that seems to be the key: they don't follow their emotions over a cliff into poor decision-making and panic.

They simply pause and get curious.

What would a world look like where, instead of relentlessly focusing on the small proportion of topics we disagree about, we could take a deep dive into what we can agree upon *together*?

## What if, in every area of friction, we started focusing on finding the answer to the question, "What do we *both* want more of?"[26]

Who knows what is possible then!

What if when we felt most angry, scared, or agitated we tried getting curious about one another and asking better questions about each other's experiences? Questions that help us step into somebody else's shoes or find places where we are similar? This might point the way to realizing we need each other to create a positive human experience. Asking better questions when we are in a heightened state of emotion keeps us from falling into the division that was leading us further into darkness.

I believe we are at a point in human history that calls us to pause.

## Pause and shift from contempt to curiosity.

Our highly refined skills for swift *confrontation, blame, and critique* are getting us nowhere but further down the path of contempt. And contempt leads to one of the most unproductive human emotions: outrage. How many times have we seen outrage lead to catastrophic results – irreparably broken relationships, lost jobs, or even lost lives?

I believe we have got to address *the cycle of contempt* that leads to outrage, or we are in for an even more frightening ride.

Curiosity is the antidote to contempt. I suspect it is just the right medicine for our times, and it will reveal unimaginable rewards for all of us.

Like learning any new skill, shifting our mindset from contempt to curiosity takes practice. It is not reserved for life-long optimists, cheerful grandmas with a sunny attitude, or the perpetually kind. We all can get there, and when we do we'll find that this hard-won habit pays off in unimaginable ways.

In the new era, most of us will applaud the bridge-builders who can stay curious, and the *chaos-builders* will begin to look very out of step.

I can assure you that I am not looking at the world with rose-colored glasses. It's just that I'm very careful about what I give my attention to, and I'm always rewarded with some nugget of insight or wisdom when I shift from contempt to curiosity as quickly as possible.

Sometimes, I listen to the way all sides carry on about their disagreements, and I'm left shaking my head. No wonder we are so mired and can't make progress on the things that would make the world a better place for everyone. We are spending most of our energy on ratcheting up the contempt and never spending a minute talking about all that we have in common and what we all want!

In other words, we never start with our strengths. When you consider this on a human-to-human level you will see that it makes no sense.

Think of it this way: When we go out with someone the first couple of times, whether it's a date or just coffee with a new friend, we don't talk about our deep issues involving our mother or the things that make us outraged.

Instead, it's all about discovering what we have in common, laughing at the serendipity in our experiences that overlap, and talking excitedly about what gives us wonder and joy. It's about being curious about one another. There's a thrill of possibility in all that listening and connecting. If you are lucky and you both mind the rules of *give and take* in conversation, it can be absolutely magical.

It's only later, once we have an established relationship that we drop in a few comments that might be a smidge contentious. We test the waters and back off immediately if we feel some friction, because by date number three we have found so much that we have in common and we don't want to trade all of that away for one sticking point. After all, a seventy or eighty percent match seems too precious to waste in this world that can be very complex, draining, and lonely.

We understand that the contentious stuff can wait until our relationship can stand up to a little dip in energy. Once we've invested some time in uncovering the many things we have in common, we can place the right level of emphasis and priority on the things we disagree on.

The same could be said of society as a whole: our commonalities are too precious to waste in a world so complex. Of course we rarely hear anyone in the news or on social media celebrating those commonalities, or the times we have used them as a force for good.

So let's do that. Let's zoom back out and study what happens when we apply that recipe for relationship-building to the larger society. It wouldn't be the first time humans have successfully used this curiosity/give and take cycle!

- Did you know that in 1985, one hundred ninety-three countries came together and were able to start radically closing the hole in the ozone layer[27] that aerosol and refrigerant chemicals had created? We saved our planet together, and almost no one knows about it! Look it up. The story is astounding.

- Did you know that in 1980, we celebrated wiping the deadly smallpox virus (which had killed three hundred million people in the twentieth century alone[28]) off the face of the earth? The facts on that feat of unity are extraordinary too, and yet the whole story is fading to obscurity.

- Just look at the scale of global generosity[29] that appeared after the 2004 tsunami killed over 280,000 people in fourteen countries in Southeast Asia and, for that matter, the generosity that appears after almost every major natural disaster.

I could go on.

People can come together.

No one was asking about others' politics when they rescued their neighbors off porches and rooftops during the flooding in New Orleans in 2005 or Houston in 2017. No one was calling into the rubble after the earthquake in Haiti, asking about people's political views before they began to dig them out.

People just did what they could do for each other.

In fact, I think I saw a lot of that same sort of relationship-building going on through the lead-up to the quarantines and then again through social distancing. A lot of people got really clever and flexible, and our priorities changed! We started seeing people in the media and those conducting business from their homes shedding their façade of perfection and doing what they could to get the job done. We saw them wearing baseball caps because their hair, like ours, was overgrown and out of shape. We saw their small children racing through the house screaming, just like ours. We saw a lot of peoples' kitchens as backdrops and they looked a lot like ours.

There was a shift in our perspectives. People were suddenly thrust into a new reality: *We are all in this together, folks!*

This chapter in history is asking us to do just what our mothers and grandmothers told us to do when we needed to make a situation better: try to feel what it would be like to walk in someone else's shoes.

One by one, we realized that we are not so different and we are now dependent upon the thoughtfulness of others.

Ordinary people are leading progress too!

A chapter about *"who we will become"* would not be complete without some examples of the wisdom and generosity of ordinary people from the Conspiracy of Goodness of our times. Both before and after the social upheaval of the pandemic, there was no end to the cleverness and kindness to be found. In fact, we want to shine a light on the people changing our neighborhoods and communities, because that's where all goodness and progress starts to take root.

And eventually, *being kinder than we need to be* becomes just how it's done.

When we get it right, we can feel it beaming from others.

*Here I am with some nuns in a remote part of Tibet who radiate the kind of goodness we can cultivate in a new era if we carefully choose what to give our attention to.*

Here are some examples of a groundswell of ordinary people solving small but important problems with their own two hands well before the pandemic.

## Dadarao Bilhore – Pothole Life Saver

What would your response be to the loss of a child? For Dadarao Bilhore, who lost his son in a pothole-related car accident in India, his response was to do something about the problem that took his son's life. In 2017, potholes were the cause of at least ten deaths a day in India.[30] Using a mix of easily found materials and just the right technique, Dadarao took it upon himself to fill six hundred potholes,[31] and counting. His work and commitment to his community has single-handedly saved hundreds of lives.

*"When you do something noble and beautiful and nobody notices, do not be sad. For the sun every morning is a beautiful spectacle and yet most of the audience still sleeps."*

*– John Lennon*

## Napping Brother from Saint Norbert Abbey and the Cat Shelter

This is one of my favorite recent examples of ordinary people just doing what they can do. It is the story of a retired teacher (and brother from Saint Norbert Abbey) of Green Bay[32] who started visiting the local Safe Haven Pet Sanctuary, a 501(c)(3) no-kill, cage-free cat sanctuary and rehabilitation center that rescues kitties with special needs. Eventually he started falling asleep on a big overstuffed couch, covered in cats, and the staff would take heartwarming, often funny, photos of him napping. The shelter then created a Cat Grandpa 2020 Calendar, and it has raised over one hundred thousand dollars for the shelter.[33]

Now that's taking something you are good at and putting it to good use!

It makes me think of those Seven Rescuers from the Conspiracy of Goodness story again.

# What if the Seven Rescuers in the story of the Conspiracy of Goodness decided

# not to help? What if the Dutch rescuer had not had the help of the mailman, the milkman, and the neighbors?

We can all do something that's helpful. We each have the potential to be one of the Seven Rescuers in the Conspiracy of Goodness in our times.

*"Do what you can, with what you have, where you are."*

*— Theodore Roosevelt*

### Busker Gives His Money Away[34]

And then there is the NYC busker, Will Boyajian,[35] who sings and plays his guitar in the subway and has a big sign telling people in need that they can TAKE his money!

Yes, ordinary people put money in this guy's guitar case so he can then be a conduit, passing it on to those who are dealing with hardships. Some of the stories he tells are absolutely wonderful.

He has reimagined busking and found an ingenious way to help. And it is a win/win for everyone. What else can we reimagine?

# My best advice: SEEK Signs of Goodness and Progress, and you will start noticing it popping up everywhere!

## It's up to us to get those balls rolling by "sharing" the good intention and progress for all when we are seeing it.

I believe we can bring *thoughtfulness* back into fashion, and the four simple shifts that I'm suggesting can serve you and everyone you come in contact with. From the minute you put this book down, you will start seeing all that we have in common and how we can use it to spread goodness and progress for everyone.

This goodness is out there just waiting to bubble up from the quiet, undiscovered corners of the internet and news media. In the *Gratitude Economy* that is coming, the best thought leaders will be those who are supporting goodness and helping to reveal it to the world.

One of the most important questions we can ask ourselves these days is:

## How can we reward and give our attention to people who are being helpful?

Can we bring that way of being back into fashion too?

# CHAPTER ELEVEN

# The Gratitude Economy

Throughout this book I've talked about how you can take actions that impact the world, but what about the broader picture and massive influence the corporate world wields over it? Well, that's changing too! Businesses are also getting in on the Conspiracy of Goodness, though in many cases their decisions begin with the actions of individuals like me and you.

## There is a "Gratitude Economy" coming.

Have you noticed how many millennials use their purchasing power to show gratitude for the innovators and problem-solvers? They are voting with their wallets, and they are not alone; many people from all generations are starting to put their money where their values are.

I started thinking not only about my own experience, but those of my friends. I noticed they were giving more thought to their purchasing, so I did a little research to see if I could find evidence of a larger pattern. Sure enough, I found a study[36] that concluded that sixty-four percent of consumers now self-identify as "Belief-Driven Buyers"; in other words, "...they use brands to demonstrate their personal values. They will choose, switch, avoid or boycott a brand based on where it stands on the political or social issues they care about." This was a 13-point increase from the previous year, which is huge when one considers how hard it is to move the needle on social concepts.

It also seems we are changing what we expect from our employer! A 2019 study by Glassdoor[37] found that people want to work for companies that share their values.

Here's an acronym you are going to hear a lot about in the future: CSR (Corporate Social Responsibility.[38]) More and more, we expect the big players to use money and influence to make the world a better place.

Corporations know a new ecosystem is developing for business, and they are creating divisions devoted to giving back.[39]

Did you know that Lego Corporation has committed to making all products and packaging from sustainable materials by 2025[40]? Or that the UPS Foundation[41] is supporting a start-up company that uses drones to fly life-saving blood and vaccines to remote corners of Africa?

The famous global fashion label Marc Jacobs[42] has committed to helping The Sato Project relocate dogs abandoned on "Dead Dog Beach" in Puerto Rico, so named because the area has no food or water, and people just drop unwanted dogs off there to die.

Those are a few of the major players contributing to the wave of goodness that is beginning to usher in a new era.[43] But there is an even more delightful wave of business progress happening at the start-up level!

There used to be two major categories for people deciding to start a business: for profit or non-profit. These days, you may have noticed a rising business trend where people start "for profit" businesses that have an aspect of social change at the core of their work. These are referred to as "Mission-Driven For-Profit" businesses, which have become a welcomed addition to the global economy.

Look around, and you'll start to see these mission-driven businesses everywhere. They are built to make the world a better place AND pay their bills!

At Ever Widening Circles, we have pointed people to a number of them in our gift-giving guides. Five North Chocolate,[44] for example, is an amazing company that is making the world a better place by carefully managing every detail of how chocolate finds its way into our mouths. Did you know that much of the world's chocolate production involves dreadful practices like child labor and rampant deforestation?[45] Well, some of the biggest names in that industry have promised to end all that, only to end up breaking those promises. Five North Chocolate helps to address those shortfalls by committing to taking the guilt out of our favorite treats.

GroFive[46] is a company that is saving hundreds of thousands of children simply by putting shoes on their feet. Did you know that 300 million children in the world go without shoes, and are therefore especially vulnerable to soil-transmitted diseases and parasites that can disable or kill them? Enter Kenton Lee and his company, GroFive. GroFive is not a shoe company that added a mission statement as an afterthought. It began as a non-profit with a vision to create sandals that grow five sizes with children's feet.

Eventually, they received so many notes from people who wanted to buy their shoes that they created *Expandals*,[47] to satisfy the demand and support the GroFive mission!

RoHo[48] is another great example of how our purchases can help directly support communities around the world. Your RoHo purchase supports the work of more than four hundred Kenyan artisans, helping to feed their families and send their children to school.

While searching for ethical, forward-thinking companies to purchase from, don't forget to check out the home-grown ingenuity in your own backyard. One of my favorite local businesses in our area is Bellcate School Dog Treats.[49] Bellcate is a remarkable school that works with students with a wide range of learning needs. Their dog treats business helps students with special needs develop business and employment skills. We are big fans of theirs, and Finn, the Ever Widening Circles dog, *loves* these treats! Once you start recognizing these local gems in your own community, support them and you will start seeing them everywhere.

These are just a few of the examples I've seen of people who are looking at problems and diving in, rather than just pulling the covers over their heads.

I recently met Hope Zvara, a wonderful woman who partnered with fellow Wisconsin entrepreneur Phil Knuckey to start Mother Trucker Yoga,[50] a company that helps drivers in the trucking industry move in the direction of better health. They've created a series of three- to five-minute, easy-to-follow videos that teach truckers how to do yoga while on the road – stretches while they wait for their gas tanks to fill up and poses they can do in their cab before bed. Their mission to help everyone "feel better, wherever!" is a win/win. They are helping thousands of hardworking people while also making a good living.

By sharing what we know with those who need it, we can make great change in the world while also paying our own bills. Good intention and good business are not opposite sides of the coin. We are already seeing how these types of enterprises can lead us into the future.

Keep your eye out for small businesses that are working with a social responsibility model, then watch how large they become. Have you ever made a decision about where to buy eyeglasses, shoes, or socks based on a particular brand's efforts to do good in the world? Think Warby Parker[51] eyeglasses, TOMS shoes,[52] and Bombas socks.[53] All three of these big companies were founded on the principle that doing good in the world can be good business. That "buy one and we'll give one to someone in need" model is proving to be a win/win recipe in many markets, and there is a whole generation coming up that is willing to pay a little more to companies that are genuinely interested in giving back.

And many businesses are taking notice.

## So how do we know who to trust?

Before supporting a mission-driven project, business, or cause, you have to do some quick homework to make sure they are trustworthy. Here's my quick routine:

First, I look at the "About" page. Do they look like real people, or does the page feel like it's been written by a computer or marketing firm? I am wary of About pages that don't make me feel like I know and understand why someone is on the mission.

Then, if they have a board of advisors (most non-profits will), I take a solid look at the members. You can Google them separately as individuals and see their digital footprint on the web (Google the name of the founder while you are at it!). Do these people look responsible, trustworthy, and in a good position to help make the world a better place?

Since everyone has a digital footprint these days, it doesn't even take me five minutes to track down those details. Most are going to be fine, but you never know until you look.

Here's why I got into the habit of doing a little homework before I give someone my time or money. After the earthquake in Haiti, an employee asked me to help her finance her trip there so she could help with the relief effort. She told me she had found an organization charging two thousand dollars a week to host volunteers. Something didn't seem quite right, so I did a little research on the founder. It turned out that he and his wife had previously been involved with a business that swindled people, and they had both spent time in prison.

That was a rare case, but those kinds of people are out there and it's easy to weed them out if you take five to ten minutes to do a little sleuthing. You'll find that most of the time this research turns out fine and gets you even more inspired to help! My guiding principle is: *Are the people I'm thinking of supporting the kind of people I would love to have as neighbors?* If I cannot tell that from the website, it gives me pause and warrants more due diligence.

Next, I look at the blog and social media accounts. When was the last time they updated them? This will tell you if an organization is even still active (believe it or not, seventy percent of the sites on the web are not!)[54]. The social media pages also indicate if they are making headway, so when they have something to celebrate you should be able to find it somewhere.

## If you want to truly understand someone or quickly measure the good intention of an organization or project, look at what they celebrate.

Look at their social media from that angle, and you will learn a lot about what they value! If they are celebrating examples of how their team won the last political skirmish by putting someone in their place or with ridicule that offends people's dignity, or if they celebrate an opponent "losing it" or use emotionally charged words like "we mopped the floor with them" or "go pound sand," it's pretty easy to see that what they celebrate is division.

## What we celebrate defines us.

This is an excellent quick tip to help you decide who to trust with your attention. If much of what you see coming from an influencer or organization is about winners and losers, fear and outrage, then division is clearly a priority and I suspect their influence will be fading in the coming era. People are becoming exhausted by acrimony.

For many of us, it is like we are trying to think clearly while a fire alarm is constantly blaring.

On the other hand, if your search uncovers an organization that seems to celebrate discovery, collaboration, creativity, community, beauty, and self-reflection, then you've probably found a winner.

Here's the bottom line:

There is a new era coming, one in which the new social currency will be gratitude.

We will all be grateful for the people and businesses keeping a cool head, bringing us all together, celebrating what we can do together, and pointing to possibilities we never imagined. They are part of the Conspiracy of Goodness of our times.

And we will reward *THEM* with our attention.

# CHAPTER TWELVE

## The Recipe for the New Era

Now that you understand the four shifts, I want to show you how they play out in the day-to-day efforts of people who are solving problems, and in the end we will see how we can incorporate some of their methods into our own lives. As I've learned from writing about these innovators, there appears to be some common themes in the way they do things that can serve as hallmarks for what our world needs most right now: collaboration and imagination.

Maybe those two elements would help you in your personal life right now? Has your life become immeasurably complex in some way?

The most promising endeavors we've written about have five characteristics that align them squarely with the Conspiracy of Goodness of our times. I'm calling this "The Innovator's Recipe." To my mind, they are good predictors of impact, and I personally use them *every day* to address something that needs attention.

1. **Source:** After rigorous study and intention, they get as close to the origin of the problem as possible in order to devise a solution. They peel back the onion until a root cause appears.

2. **Creative:** They put concepts together that no one has ever thought to combine.

3. **Surplus:** Their solution involves things they already have in surplus. (It doesn't require them to create more stuff.)

4. **Collaborate:** The solution involves communities of people in an imaginative way to find a win/win for everyone.

5. **Lead with Grace:** The leader is a bridge-builder who works hard to avoid creating enemies.

Makes complete sense when you think about it, doesn't it?

Unfortunately, groups and individuals often expend a lot of energy working in directions that are in direct contradiction to these five concepts. For example:

1. We often see a problem and address it directly without uncovering the source, so the problem persists even after all our efforts.

2. We often try to sharpen the same approach we've been using repeatedly, instead of thinking outside the box completely.

3. When we react to problems with a knee-jerk idea, we often move in the direction of creating all kinds of new infrastructure, without looking at what we already have in abundance that could be useful.

4.  And most commonly, we forget to include the very people we are trying to serve in our solutions.

5.  And that last point – leading with grace – is the one that can really sink the ship. If we have to create enemies while coming up with our solutions, then there is going to be too much energy bearing down on our fledgling idea for it to survive.

Next time you see a public figure or "influencer" pontificating about their ideas for the future, see if what they are proposing aligns with the five parts of The Innovator's Recipe. We've looked at the work of thousands of thought leaders, and the ones who are likely to change the future in a good way, and help open a new era, are the ones who match that five-part profile.

An excellent example of this is The Rainforest Connection,[55] [56] which as mentioned earlier, utilizes modern technology to stop illegal deforestation.

If I only had room to tell you about one thought leader in the enormous wave of progress in our times, it would have to be Topher White and his solution to save the remaining rainforests in the world.

Topher's work rises to the top because he exemplifies those five characteristics that will be common to the most successful ideas in the upcoming era. After looking closely at the wonder in Topher's endeavor, you will be able to easily start recognizing this recipe for success (or the absence of it) in your world.

# Topher White and the Rainforest Connection[57]

Topher was an engineer vacationing in Borneo when he had his *ah-ha!* moment. During a visit to a gibbon sanctuary, the staff suddenly stopped what they were doing and ran into the forest in the direction of a faint sound. Topher followed and was astonished to realize that a short distance from the sanctuary, in a protected region of forest, illegal loggers were taking down an enormous tree. The normal rainforest sounds had almost completely muffled the sounds of their chainsaws.

Topher's life was changed forever, and since then he has dedicated himself to finding a way to solve the problem of rainforest destruction.

Why should we care? Well, in my research for an article about Topher's work, I learned that deforestation is responsible for releasing more $CO_2$ into the atmosphere than all the world's cars and trucks put together.[58] That's such an astounding fact. How come we don't all know this?!

But here's the good news: Topher has devised an ingenious way to end illegal logging using the old cell phones that many of us have thrown in a junk drawer. He and his team tune them to pick up only the frequency of the sound of a chainsaw, and then they are placed at intervals in the forest canopy to relay information across vast distances, and powered by their own tiny arrays of solar collectors.

The minute a chainsaw is fired up, the phones send a signal that alerts forest rangers who can swoop in to stop the illegal loggers!

Topher estimated that one device in a tree can help protect three square kilometers of rainforest. "That equals taking three thousand cars off the road..."[59] Imagine this solution at scale around the world!

And the innovation just keeps coming. After working with the Cornell Department of Ornithology, the Rainforest Connection team[60] realized that the birds of the rainforest start to make different noises when a logger enters the forest. So now the phones are set to detect that change and forest rangers can arrive before the chainsaws are even started!

At scale, Topher may have the solution to solving *twenty-three percent* of our greenhouse gas problem.[61] And again I have to ask, "Why don't we all know about this innovation?"

We would, if we knew that we could ignore the chaos and use our clicks as votes to make progress like this rise to the top of the internet and news.

Now, in order to see how you can evaluate which projects are worth your support (and start using those five parts in your own problem-solving efforts), let's put the Rainforest Connection's solution to deforestation through a microscope and see why it so perfectly fits the future model of success.

1. **Source:** They attack the problem of deforestation at its most fundamental starting point: where the chainsaw meets the tree trunk. If you can't put a chainsaw to the trees, the trees are not coming down.

2. **Creative:** They put together two things that no one ever thought to combine: old cell phones and rainforests. They realized that using smartphone technology to listen from the forest canopy would yield a trove of information about how illegal loggers reveal themselves as they are getting access to the trees. Then they put together two new things: bird songs and satellite technology.

3. **Surplus:** They came up with an idea that uses things we already have a lot of: old phones, sitting in junk drawers around the

world. They did not need to build out more infrastructure, and they needed no new cell towers. The trees are their towers!

4. **Collaborate:** The Rainforest Connection realized that every remaining rainforest in the world is surrounded by communities that are seeing their way of life under siege. In Brazil, for example, twenty percent of the Amazon rainforest has been set aside for indigenous people (their intactness has in fact made them the target of illegal loggers and poachers). Because of their local knowledge and all they have at stake, the villagers are the ideal collaboration partners.

5. **Graceful Leaders:** We have observed that the most promising insights and innovations are championed by someone who has a natural gift for bringing people together. They seem to have no interest at all in engaging their enemies; rather, they are such endearing and inspiring people that we naturally want to follow and support them. I had a beer with Topher White one evening, and he was a delight: quietly passionate, approachable, and super nice.

The Rainforest Connection has all five characteristics in spades; it also demonstrates why we need to know more about the Topher Whites of the world. Remember that period in the fall of 2019, when all we saw on the news was the rainforests burning in Brazil? While I'm as crushed as anyone by those news stories, I can hold that feeling in one hand and hope in the other simply because I know about the thought leaders like Topher who are out there working on solutions to our biggest problems.

Oliver Percovich's skateboarding project in Afghanistan (which I spoke about in Chapter 8) also follows this recipe and gives me the same sense of hope when I hear some dreadful piece of news about Afghanistan. The same thing happens when I see an upsetting news story about plastics in the ocean. I think of the many organizations and individuals in the zero-waste movement who also follow this recipe for success.

We can all go straight to the Source of the problem, make Creative Connections using things we have in Surplus, and Collaborate with everyone involved. And, as Graceful Leaders, we can be approachable people, building bridges.

In problem solving, large and small, we can be *the helpers* that the world needs now.

# CHAPTER THIRTEEN

# Look for the Helpers

I have the sense that we are at a great tipping point in society.

The "influencers" in the new era will be people whose ideas create remarkable new ways of looking at what is possible.

They will be the "helpers," the ones who are asking better questions that open completely new doors to possibility. Most importantly, they will be complaining less and collaborating more. Instead of fighting for their team, they will be fighting for ideas that can translate into real progress for everyone.

The thought leaders in a new era will be the ones who can look at the quandary we are in and synthesize stakeholders' key interest into a plan. They are out there by the thousands. Their ideas will be scalable and replicable, without their personal involvement. You will recognize them because ego, shaming, and division will be missing from the equation when you hear them speak.

## The thought leaders in the Gratitude Economy will be the people who can de-escalate tension and drama, while still making progress.

These go-to people will not be the loudest voices. They will be those who have proven track records of rigorous, good intention, collaboration, and curiosity. They will be multipliers for ideas in areas that seem completely unrelated, but *that* will be their genius.

They will be the ones who can connect things no one ever thought to combine.

At Ever Widening Circles we've pointed to the work of thousands across an enormous span of the human experience. There is the tattoo artist who changes hateful tattoos to artistic wonders[62] for people who have had a change of heart. There is the project that demonstrates that we can grow the equivalent of a two-acre garden in one shipping container.[63] There are organizations using dogs to detect signs of seizures in humans before they happen.[64] There is a remarkably insightful kind of kindergarten where the children *never* go indoors, for any reason. There is the doctor who found a way to restore sight to the blind with a three-dollar innovation.[65] I could go on and on.

# After writing about so many of these innovators, I'm beginning to think that almost every challenge we face stems from one simple problem: a lack of imagination.

Some of the most creative solutions in the coming era will come from "outsiders," people who bring perspectives from completely unrelated fields and can inspire huge leaps in tackling our world's most vexing problems.

Here's one of the best examples:

Damien Mander is an amazing thought leader in the field of saving endangered species. He has discovered that, for a host of reasons, single mothers make the very best game wardens in Africa, benefitting wildlife, communities, and generations. His organization, The Akashinga Initiative,[66] is a perfect example of how we will be expanding our view of who and what is helpful in the coming era.

I stumbled upon Damien a few years ago after I saw a news story saying that the last male northern white rhino on the planet had died.[67] I remember a particularly sharp, sinking feeling, like a foundation of some sort was crumbling. Exterminating an entire species from the planet points to a level of ignorance that does not bode well for our own species.

Fortunately, I've learned that the best antidote for bad news is to SEEK signs of goodness and progress related to that particular story. Sure enough, I discovered Damien's amazing organization[68] that is using a counter-intuitive model to protect endangered wildlife in Africa, and with great success.

Here's where Damien's status as an outsider to wildlife conservation becomes valuable: He's an Australian former military sniper who, after his stint as a counter-insurgency specialist in Iraq, discovered that his experience might be useful in the war against wildlife poaching.[69] (He describes this journey in his 2013 TED Talk[70]; I found it to be one of the most powerful call-to-action Ted Talks out there.) What has transpired since then has gone way beyond his original modest ambitions.

His efforts began in Africa's Zambezi River Valley, where he trained conventional (male) game wardens in the rigorous techniques from his counterinsurgency background. To his dismay, it was a complete failure. At the end of his first training session, only three of the one-hundred-twenty-plus rangers remained.

Damien also realized that his approach was not sustainable. Though they had made some anti-poaching progress in Mozambique, it had also resulted in an escalating, full-on war with organized crime. There was something amiss at the foundational level that failed to get to the source of the problem.

After going back to the drawing board, he decided to try an experiment: training young women. He found that they stuck with his uncompromising training program and washed out in very small numbers! They were also far better at de-escalation with criminal elements, in part because of their skill at gathering information locally that headed off disaster. The experiment also revealed another interesting fact: of his female trainees, single mothers were the most successful.

Specifically, Damien and his team discovered four amazing advantages to this new model:[71]

- Female game wardens more consistently use their earnings to improve the lives of the people around them. A woman with a salary in rural Africa invests up to three times more than a male into their family.
- They are looked upon with high esteem, which attracts others and makes the project sustainable.
- This new way of doing things fosters harmonious relationships with local communities as the best defense against illegal wildlife crime. Perhaps they are also less threatening and confrontational when someone in their community needs a course correction.
- It's easy to see the connection between empowering young women and inspiring their children to be better stewards and leaders as they grow up.

# One key to the very best problem-solving is the notion of bringing it all back to "community," where all lasting change actually takes place.

There are so many insights and innovations in this one project. It exemplifies the truism that at the heart of every success story are solutions that support surrounding communities, instead of alienating them. Damien's story is also an example of the remarkable untapped potential in society's most disenfranchised groups. It shows the incredible things we can achieve when we are willing to turn over new rocks in our search for solutions.

If we run the Akashinga success story through our Innovator's Recipe, they too come through as a shining example of how progress will be made in the coming Gratitude Economy. They start with the source of the problem – desperate poverty – then make Creative Connections using resources we have in Surplus, and Collaborate with everyone involved. Lastly, as a part of our 5-point recipe, Damien has assembled an advisory committee of true bridge-builders that includes the indomitable Jane Goodall. You may know her by her pioneering work studying wild chimpanzee communities in the 1960's and then as one of the early major thought leaders in our current wave of conservation efforts. Her good nature – graceful but firm – epitomizes the qualities of bridge-building leaders in the coming era.

Akashinga means "Brave One," and that could not be more appropriate for our times, for we will need those with courage to lead us into new places. It is the best example I can give you of the many brave people doing ingenious work that is getting lost in the chaos of the internet.

We need them to rise to the top now. We'll have to *Pause*, *Ignore* more, *Seek* them out and *Share* their stories and they will surely become part of a new dialogue about the future.

Rather than disputing, we could be discovering.

It's all about what we seek.

Search for missed potential and you will almost always find it. Search for something positive about someone and you will almost always discover it.

But here's the secret: Discovery will only flourish when we de-escalate the tension and drama.

And here's how we do that: We stop talking about *individuals* as barriers to progress and start talking about the *behaviors* that limit our ability to think together.

Remember, the actions that are building the chaos in our world are those that unintentionally or intentionally trigger our most impulsive emotions – aggression, shame, fear, scarcity. We need to give our attention to thought leaders who are being more thoughtful before they speak. The ones who are not leading us over a cliff of emotion.

To put a finer point on that, there are some wonderful, loud voices who we like and who have the best of intentions, yet who are also engaging in some serious chaos-building. I was once one of them: passionate, fearless, quick to call out injustice, quick to mistake inaction for apathy. And I know some extraordinarily good people who are adding to the chaos that same way. Most have a life of experiences that fuels their fiery responses. Some are lovely, amazingly passionate, and fair-minded people.

## This is the quandary of our times:

## Many of the chaos-builders see a problem and want to fix it; unfortunately, our current system forces them to shout about it.

## We need a new system.

## I suspect it will start with discovering what we all have in common.

## But ratcheting up the drama as a way of addressing an issue just doesn't feel helpful or thoughtful anymore. It's adding to the sense of overwhelm and leaving many good people silent and apathetic.

I want to reiterate: I love people with passion. When I refer to the chaos-building, I'm referring to a behavior, *not* the person.

No matter how you slice it, escalating the tension and drama in a situation rarely gets to the best outcome. It's a nasty cycle. And it's time to reimagine a new way forward that does not include aggression, shaming, and fear.

Many, if not most, of us are tired of being shouted at from all corners. We are tired of being shamed for not doing enough. The hype and constant din of doom and gloom has left us emotionally exhausted. To use another familiar analogy, sometimes it feels like we are trying to think clearly with a screaming baby in our arms! It can't be done. If you've been there, you know that in that state of mind, your haste to stop the noise can create more of a mess than what you started with.

Have you noticed that politicians waving their arms, shouting, and pointing while making a point is starting to feel a bit off-putting, even if you are on the same team? That way of appealing to our emotions (i.e. outrage and alarm) is a part of the chaos that often deepens divisions and ignores what binds us.

My goal is to bring us together and have us each take an honest look at our role in the chaos-building, no matter where we start.

We can be forgiven for letting it all hang out on social media up to now, but we need to pause. There are people whose job it is to trigger our worst impulses, and some are very good at that work!

Maybe you've been able to resist all that, and the only thing you have to do after reading this book is start withholding your clicks from the chaos-

# builders. Or, maybe your Twitter feed is only adding to the drama.

# Either way, I'm with you. This is a journey, and we are all in this together.

And since I am uninterested in adding to the chaos myself, the only thing I will do is ask others to start using their "inside voices," like we were taught in kindergarten. I'm going to call on all of us to pause, get curious, and search for a solution that does *not* add to the overwhelm and anxiety in society.

I'm going to keep on believing that everyone has a piece of the puzzle and that we can put together something new if we look at everyone else's experiences and opinions as valuable.

We are where we are.

I suspect it's time to create a new social contract about what's helpful and what is not.

Change is coming, and it doesn't have to involve winners and losers.

Even the people who make a living triggering our negative impulses can shift (and thrive) if we demonstrate our support and flock to thought leaders who change division to discovery. In fact, I believe some of the most divisive voices in the media could redirect their messaging if we protected their dignity and validated their experiences. Most importantly, people need the space to search for clarity and change their minds.

I look forward to being interviewed by some of them one day. When I watch how passionate some of the most divisive people in the media are, it leaves me curious about the personal experience behind those reactions. You don't get the heart of a lion without a major test in your youth. And the stories of those kinds of tests always improve my way of thinking.

Now, we have "thoughtful" and "helpful" to stand on as we usher in a new era.

This is who we are. This is who we have always been through thousands of years of human history.

*"When I was a boy, I would see scary things on the news, my mother would say to me, 'Look for the helpers. You will always find people helping.'"*

*— Mr. Rogers*

# CHAPTER FOURTEEN

# From Contempt to Curiosity

Have you ever tossed a pebble into the water, then watched as ripples started to form outward, one after another? These are ever-widening circles that can be a constant reminder of our individual importance in the scheme of things. Every word and deed has the power to change the future in some way, large and small.

I can now imagine a world where many, if not most, people realize that. The pandemic and upheaval have forced us to practice a new brand of self-control. And way more often, most of us are consciously pausing and thinking before we speak and act.

That's what makes the worst of times work at a fundamental level. We realize the potential of our interconnectedness and many people rise to the occasion.

It is our appreciation of this ripple effect that inspired the name Ever Widening Circles. It is our understanding that everything we do and say affects our world, both present and future.

It has always been this way. Every kindness, every harsh word, every good deed, every compliment is just another pebble we toss into the pond.

Everything we are doing today will go out in ever widening circles and land on the shores of time.

And all those ripples will shape the children standing knee-deep in the water on those shores right now.

If for no other reason, I believe that we have to change the negative dialogue about our times for the sake of our children.

Below, I want to share with you a collage of two photos I took when I was twenty-two years old and traveling in North Africa.

The little girl in the background of both pictures was being treated like a slave in the home we visited. I have never forgotten the look in her eyes, or the mix of hopelessness and tragedy that she seemed to exude.

This chapter is for her and countless children around the world.

I believe we have reached a point in humanity when we have the ability and willingness to innovate our way out of situations like this. It is time we celebrated the unique alchemy of every child and give them each the opportunity to live into their full potential.

**We have to change the tone from Contempt to Curiosity.**

Remember, no matter how we get drawn in, we know that what we see on the internet is only a tiny slice of reality. Our children, on the other hand, have far fewer human interactions to remind them of that. They don't have any context for the frightening anger and chaos they see relentlessly on the internet and news.

Children need to have a balanced worldview if we want them to make good decisions with a positive future in mind.

I have recently begun a series of recorded conversations[72] with Linda Cliatt-Wayman (better known as Principal Cliatt-Wayman), a good friend and the woman who turned around one of the most dangerous high schools in America. In these conversations, we are discussing the wisdom of mothers and grandmothers, a space where almost everyone has some lived experiences in common, no matter their politics, generation, culture, or race.

Every time we meet to talk, we come out transformed by the context we are adding to each other's way of thinking. Perhaps this lack of context is the core of the problem with the twenty-second video or soundbite. If we have no context, there can be no understanding. We simply see or hear something, then fill in the blanks by telling ourselves a story, often one that is scary and a long way from the truth.

Recently I asked Linda what she believes is the most important thing we can do to help all children cope with situations of great turmoil and struggle. I had expected to hear a complex educational theory or a list of reforms.

Instead, she said, "Give them a reason to have hopes and dreams. Children need hope."

And she meant *all* children.

As we all know, the internet, social media, and 24-hour news cycle is probably giving them quite the opposite. But here's the good news: Children today are the first generation of "Digital Natives," meaning they have never known a world without an internet, and this makes them supremely savvy there. I'm actually excited about the possibilities once this message that "someone is counting every click you make" becomes common knowledge. These digital natives will find a way to outwit a system that's currently using their attention to manipulate and ruin their futures.

The bottom line is that young minds need evidence every day to confirm that this is still an amazing world or they are going to ask the natural question, *"Why should I care?"*

And that is fundamentally the question we are answering in every Ever Widening Circles article, and with every piece on EWCed, our website for students around the world.

What if they knew about remarkable innovation like the first spacecraft that needs no fuel[73] or the discovery that dogs can smell cancer before it can be picked up by normal diagnostic testing? What if children knew that trees are communicating with each other in complex ways using an underground network?

Imagine the conversations that might be sparked from a shared sense of discovery if kids were taught to connect the classroom to topics like: What Astronauts Dream About,[74] How a Blind Man Sees with Sound,[75] How Trees Communicate with Each Other,[76] Why Fruit Flies are Heroes,[77] or What Makes a Dog's Nose so Fascinating?[78]

What if teenagers knew about the insights in the most inspiring TED Talks, or about the man who is the first real cyborg[79] and is totally colorblind but now *hears* the colors of the world? What if they knew that the video game "Super Mario" could be used in schools as a great way to consider coping with adversity?

## Before we lose an entire generation, who will shape the future for all of us, we need to get the wonder in the world in front of children!

## For the sake of the children we have got to shift contempt to curiosity.

Children need us to shepherd them to a place of confident optimism. There is no chance of doing that if we continue to use the internet and social media with our lizard brain in the driver's seat. The internet is built so that fear, aggression, and outrage rise to the top and that is what our children will see in us and the world around them.

Young people need to do the business of growing up – experimenting, pushing back, trying on new personas – with the knowledge that there is at least one solid rock of composure and quiet wisdom in their lives.

You can be that rock for them. When you adjust what you see on your screens and tip the scale toward optimism within yourself, you will become an exponentially more optimistic influence for the young people around you.

You can be the one with the cool head and expanded worldview. You can see the landscape ahead more clearly and all the opportunities there, even when everyone else is seeing only roadblocks and arguing for our limitations.

## Daniel Kish and World Access for the Blind[80]

That brings me to the topic of "what's possible versus impossible." Since learning about all this human ingenuity through Ever Widening Circles and the things people are capable of, my definition of "impossible" has become very blurry. One of the earliest thought leaders who took the time to speak to me is an amazingly kind and brilliant innovator, Daniel Kish. Maybe you've heard of him? Some people call him "Bat Man."

As an infant, Daniel lost his eyes to cancer, yet he is able to "see" and has traveled the world without assistance for decades. How does a person who is completely blind see? By mastering a skill called "echo-location." Daniel uses a kind of natural sonar, much like the way bats see in the dark. And for decades he has been on a mission to travel the globe to teach his techniques to others!

Daniel started making a clicking sound when he was a toddler, and his brain adapted to use the feedback from his hearing to create mental images, or "maps," of his surroundings.

He can walk down the sidewalk in a neighborhood he's never been in and describe where all the parked cars are, the height of the bushes, how far the houses are set back from the street, what kind of fences he's passing, where the telephone poles are, how the driveways are shaped, and the size and shape of the trees!

I have spoken to him on the phone as he was navigating O'Hare Airport alone and another time as he was hiking alone on his way back from a remote cabin he visits frequently. Daniel can even ride a bike safely.

Imagine what you and I would be capable of if we just changed our definition of what's possible?

Dive into our article about Daniel's capabilities, and/or watch a wonderful video done by ABC Science from April 12, 2016 on YouTube.[81] You will feel like the door to what was once impossible has just been kicked down.

And why should we care? Well, the progress we are making in brain science will, no doubt, lead to some breathtaking leaps for humanity.

Here's another reason to reimagine how the internet could become a force for good. I believe the chaos on the web is actually crippling our ability to make rapid progress in so many areas. I recently learned about some fascinating research on human echo-location being done at a very prestigious university. Imagine my shock when the thought leader who shared this with me noted that the team doing the research did not even know Daniel Kish existed.

What!?

How fast could that kind of research progress if they had someone right in their midst who has been doing it his whole life?

And yet the people who need to connect with him haven't found him through all the chaos. The current state of the internet is burying the best and the brightest, like Daniel, who would gladly share their insights with the world.

Daniel's work reminds us how important it is to change our habits when we are on the internet.

1) **SEEK** signs of goodness and progress (the internet, for now, will not bring it to you).

2) **PAUSE** before you click on anything. Remember your click is a vote.

3) **IGNORE MORE**. We can ignore the chaos-building into obscurity.

4) **SHARE** the goodness you discover around you.

Goodness and Progress need to be discoverable. Decreasing the chaos on the internet would help us, and future generations, to imagine all that is possible. It has the potential to change the trajectory of the world.

*"From the time you were very little, you've had people who have smiled you into smiling, people who have talked you into talking, sung you into singing, loved you into loving."*

*— Mr. Rogers .*

Fred Rogers' words could not be more appropriate for our times. That's the way it's always been. We need to come together so we can do those same things now for each other and the children.

# CHAPTER FIFTEEN

# Ushering in a New Era for Yourself and Others

Now that you have a better understanding of how the internet became such a mess and how we can get out of it, it is my hope that your next venture into cyberspace will be fueled by a new view of what's possible.

Be patient with this transition. Your impulses and habits may take some time to change, as will the algorithms you've been feeding. In the meantime, and to facilitate this shift, I want you to be able to connect immediately to all the insight and innovation you can get.

Want a better world? There's an app for that!

I know that may seem self-serving. I wish there were a dozen or more places I could send you to where you would be free of ads and political agenda. Now, though, EWC is the one place that has been ever-so-carefully curating the web for insights and innovations across all fields of endeavor – Science, Arts and Culture, Sports, Technology, Nature, Curiosities – for many years with a the promise of no ads, no politics... just trustworthy sources that you can see right there, anytime you want to dive in.

I suggest that you add the EWC app to the first screen on your phone. The next time you get that "breaking news" alert, learn to pause and hit those Ever Widening Circles, then watch your worldview be transformed. The people who visit EWC regularly know that there is, indeed, an antidote for fear and dread triggered by the bad news that comes their way.

I believe that there is no better time to start a new habit of cultivating your peace of mind than this moment in human history. You have a clear choice: you can drift along, falling prey to the negative spell of the internet, or you can use these insights to make the web a powerful, positive tool in your life.

What would that world look like? What would our children think is possible for themselves if it was easy to find the best about humanity on the internet? What if just twenty-five percent of us started using the Four Shifts and allowed the internet to show us the rest of the story about ourselves and the world?

We might be ready to make that leap.

Despite what you may have seen, people today care a lot more about the suffering of others than they used to. That's why our articles about advances in science, aging well, philanthropy, nature, mental health, conservation, and ways to pull people out of poverty are so inspiring.

At EWC, we believe that in order to solve our biggest problems, our views cannot be solely defined by the negative lens of the world's problems.

This negativity is only a slice of reality, and we need to be able to see beyond that to what's *already* working. Who can we confidently follow? What is *our* role? And why should we even *care?*

The Ever Widening Circles App is the place to immediately discover stories of progress and possibility. We weave together threads of our shared humanity to help us confidently navigate this complex world.

Every visit leaves you feeling more intelligent and more connected, with a clearer understanding of *your role* in creating a brighter future.

To get you started on this new journey, I offer you this prescription:

Start every day with an Ever Widening Circles article to get your head in the world of possibility and wonder. It goes perfectly with that first cup of coffee or tea!

Enjoy how the entire Ever Widening Circles team is working to give you a personal relationship with goodness. And whatever you do, watch the videos in our articles, as they contain the magic that you will remember throughout your day and beyond.

If you find that the turmoil of our times is still getting to you, end every day with an Ever Widening Circles article, too. Let this pipeline to possibility be the last thing on your mind before bed. It will be just what the doctor ordered!

Below I share with you some personal pointers on how to use the Ever Widening Circles website so that you can begin soaring with knowledge and wonder right away. Think of these pointers as the Toll House cookie recipe – follow them and they will never fail you.

1) Check the **Read Time** we've assigned to every article and always start something you can finish. We've timed every one of our articles so you can get the greatest boost for your limited time!

    a) If you've only got twenty-three minutes left in your lunch break, or nine minutes before the kids are done with soccer practice, or forty minutes on the subway, dive into something you can actually finish and have a

HAPPINESS IS AN OPTION

beaming smile on your face for the next person you
meet.

2) Try our **SURPRISE ME** button and dive into articles that you
might not have thought you'd be interested in.

   a) Okay, I'll cut you some slack. Start with a category that
   makes your heart sing. But always leave some room for
   serendipity to expand your worldview.

   b) The things that come our way through fate are often
   what can change our future for the better. Be open.

   c) Remember, we are curating the web for insights that
   would leave people from any generation or culture
   saying, "Well, I had no idea!" Many of our fan favorites
   are on topics you would never expect, so explore!

3) We are curating the best **TED Talks.**

   a) Just type "TED Talks" in our search box and you will
   find the ones that are jaw-droppingly uplifting. When
   we find one that leaves us ALL transformed, we embed
   it in an article, write all about how the concept can
   improve our daily lives, and add some remarkable
   details about the speaker.

   b) If there is only one article you open in this category,
   make it be "Celebrate What's Right With The
   World"[82] by a thought leader who has become a great
   friend to Ever Widening Circles: renowned National
   Geographic photographer Dewitt Jones. Oh, what a
   breathtaking, funny, and game-changing talk!

4) Here's my most important tip: Do *not* skip the videos even if you say you are not a video watcher. They are included in the time we say it will take to enjoy the article.

    a)  We are a pretty darn good team of writers, but the videos contain *the* awe-inspiring spark you will never forget. That's why we chose them!

5) Travel the world with our "**Saturdays Around the World**" category. It will make your heart sing.

    a)  It's like taking an inspiring trip without ever leaving home! Those articles are full of people around the globe making their communities a better place, often in the most creative and awesome ways!

6) **Try a Circle**! That's a recommended playlist of our favorite articles with a particular topic or theme in common.

    a)  About halfway down the homepage, you find links to our latest three circles and the link to take you to the whole list!

Remember, what you give your attention to now, matters more than ever. Spend as much time as you can with the thought leaders who point to what's possible.

## This is the worst of times for so many reasons, and it can turn out to be the best of times if we use this upheaval to begin again.

Start here.

# CHAPTER SIXTEEN

## Goodness Can Be Viral Too

I am certain by now you have confirmed that you were right to keep hope burning in your heart for humanity – and the future.

Now you know why you have kept going back to the internet, hoping to find something worth taking in, some inspiration, or just a simple answer to a question.

You were right to do so, because you knew goodness and progress *must* be there somewhere.

You knew that humanity had another side that was ingenious, helpful, and measured in its approach, even though the "evidence" on the web rarely pointed to that fact.

You knew that the internet should be a source of information we can rely on when we search for irrefutable knowledge, but you realized that what you were finding was often steeped in political or commercial bias.

Your experiences in a neighborhood pond, alleyway, or forest told you

HAPPINESS IS AN OPTION

that wonder in the natural world should be easily discoverable on the internet, and shareable with your kids!

And your common sense told you that you should have been able to look up a recipe for squash without having to see that a fight about microwaves has broken out in the comments section.

**Your instincts were right to tell you that goodness and progress all had to be there somewhere, but the system just wasn't connecting you to that part of the story.**

**And now you know why: The internet – for now – is an attention economy that is favoring fear, division, and anger.**

The two most important words of that sentence are *for now*. If just twenty-five percent of us understood that our click is a vote, the internet would change, seemingly overnight. Things like good intention, honesty, ingenuity, kindness, collaboration, perseverance, empathy, and pulling together would rise to the top. We would usher in a new day.

**Imagine a world where people paused for just an instant, before they clicked, because they knew someone was counting every click they made.**

**And they asked themselves, "Do we need more of this?"**

The mediocre, meaningless, and just plain *mean* content would – by the internet's design – fall back into the same obscure places where goodness is hidden from us now.

And in that new landscape, the internet would rarely leave us feeling hopeless, and confused. Instead, it would feel like a multiplier for our best impulses. Confidence, delight, and serenity would replace the anxiety, disgust, and overwhelm we often feel now from our trips to the web.

We could all be finding good content that feels like it supports a healthy and productive life, and I suspect that's exactly what the people who built the internet were aiming for. It's there, waiting to be discovered when we start ignoring the chaos-builders and content that that turns us against each other.

Sure, there will be a small percentage of people on both extremes of every topic who will not change. In fact, when we all start ignoring internet content that strives to keep this era of division growing, they may try to shout even louder in an effort to keep the attention economy going.

But I have hope that that will eventually change, too.

There is a place in this emerging Gratitude Economy for people with strong passions and viewpoints, but the *new norm* will compel them to find better ways to communicate so that collaboration is possible.

# History tells us that there are two kinds of power in the world: money and people.

# And people always eventually get the upper hand.

We can get the upper hand on this and change the internet to a wildly positive force for progress. And to do that, we need to decide exactly what we will give our attention to. Everything on the internet lives or dies by our attention: our clicks. In the final analysis, we have all the power there.

The pandemic, while tragic in so many ways, will give us some transformative gifts. It has given us just enough time to pause and really think about how we want the next part of our lives to look and feel.

I believe we are at the end of one era and the beginning of another. And while the drama and tension may be escalating, thought leaders and helpers will appear who can show us all that we have in common, and connect ideas and people that no one ever thought to combine. That's the way the Conspiracy of Goodness has always worked, and each transition brought us to a place where we could have more joy day to day.

# I believe it is time to consider all this within the arc of time.

# When we reimagine the potential of the internet for good and change our role in it, we will end this loop of panic and outrage.

Nothing we face now or in the future can turn out well with the way we are all using the internet. As long as we don't realize that someone is counting every click we make, we will keep the fear and aggression rising to the top, and that will set the tone for the stories we are telling ourselves about each other and what's possible!

This and every other problem that comes along will be made worse until we reimagine the internet and our role in it. When we can rein this all in, our view of what's possible in the future will seem limitless. We will spend way less time searching and searching the internet for something worthwhile to take in and that will make us feel like we've gained hours in our day. And most importantly, we will not be pre-occupied with a sense of dread, worry, or overwhelm. We will be truly present and a positive force in the lives of our friends, children, co-workers, and family.

Every day, people tell me that they are just tuning out the negativity and doing what they can do to make the world around them a little better for everyone. These are often private, quiet things at first, just like the milkman, the mailman, and the neighbors of Le Chambon, France.

It's the best instinct to follow.

We do not need to be at war with each other. We can be collaborating instead of competing. We can change contempt for each other to cur-iosity and find unlimited creative solutions. I am certain that the thought leaders we have written about at Ever Widening Circles for so many years can teach us how to innovate our way right out of this dark era.

We can use our differences as the wild mix of ingredients in the recipe for win/win solutions, and we will move forward.

The Four Shifts are a *crack of light* under the door right now, but after a time, if you follow them tenaciously, you will grow to feel invincible and that will radiate outward to others.

What would a world look like where, instead of relentlessly focusing on the small proportion of topics we disagree about, we could take a deep dive into what we can agree upon *together*?

What if, in every area of friction, we started focusing on finding the answer to the question, "What do we *both* want more of?"[83]

Who knows what is possible then!

What if when we felt most angry, scared, or agitated, we became curious about one another and asked better questions about each other's experiences? What questions might help us step into somebody else's shoes or find places where we are similar? This might point the way to realizing we need each other to create a positive human experience. Asking better questions when we are in a heightened state of emotion keeps us from falling into the division that was leading us further into darkness.

I believe we are at a point in human history that calls us to pause.

Pause and shift from contempt to curiosity.

Our highly refined skills for swift *confrontation, blame, and critique* are getting us nowhere but further down the path of contempt. And contempt leads to one of the most unproductive human emotions: *outrage.* How many times have we seen outrage lead to catastrophic results – irreparably broken relationships, lost jobs, or even lost lives?

What if we spread the word that a click is like a vote? What if people understood that clicking in ABC mode – Anger, Boredom, or random Curiosity – actually brings us all more negativity and chaos? What if we started purposefully sharing content that points to a brighter shared future?

That can all happen now. I know the world we would wake up to every morning would make us feel like anything is possible.

Our Ever Widening Circles journey has taught us that there is no end to the people and projects aimed specifically at improving the future for everyone. We just need to know about them. And now you know how to see that more and more each day:

**SEEK** signs of goodness and progress (the internet, for now, will not bring it to you).

**PAUSE** before you click on anything. Your click is a vote.

**IGNORE MORE.** We can ignore the chaos-building into obscurity.

**SHARE** the goodness you discover around you.

With those four simple shifts you will re-train the algorithms that are serving you the next thing you see on the internet. And you will be sending content creators a strong message that you will support positive internet content and ignore everything that is not helpful and thoughtful.

And then, start having more real conversations about possibility, with your friends, your kids, and your co-workers.

We need to start telling ourselves a new story.

That's the aim of all we are doing at Ever Widening Circles: to be a reliable place that points to stories of progress and possibility for us all. Happiness is an option. We can thrive (instead of just surviving) in the age of the internet. And now you know how.

In closing, I'd like to share one last story to consider as you begin your efforts to find more joy and positive possibilities.

In the summer of 2019, I was in Kibera, Kenya, one of the largest and most dangerous slums in the world, interviewing the members of an amazing group of artists.

In Kibera, raw sewage runs in the streets and only twenty-five percent of its 500,000-plus people have access to electricity. All the structures are pieced together with mud and reused pieces of metal and wood. For hundreds of thousands of residents, there is no infrastructure for public services, so carrying a machete on your hip is practical common sense.

And yet, when I asked some of the artists if they thought the future was hopeless, each would pause, smiled broadly, and then shared an amazing list of things that ordinary people are doing in Kibera to make the future brighter there! Most of them involved the children.

This was an inspiring moment of clarity for me.

## Progress is all about perspective, and perspective is about the stories we tell ourselves.

Those artists were not looking around and seeing the obstacles, telling themselves what can't be done. They were dialed-in to finding every possible window of opportunity that existed.

Here's a picture of my good friends during this wonderful moment of connection and possibility together:

I hope they have stayed safe. They were choosing to focus on discovery and collaboration. They were very consciously choosing what to give their attention to.

If they can do it, we all can, too.

It's a model that could be repeated anywhere in the world.

Knowing more about the wave of progress in our times can change every decision you make and every interaction you have, and we all know that kind of good intention goes out in ever widening circles.

It is going to be okay.

It is *still* an amazing world.

# ABOUT THE AUTHOR

Dr. Lynda M. Ulrich has been a business leader, global traveler, artist, and innovator her whole life.

From her earliest experiences, Dr. Lynda learned to seek goodness around her, demand it when it was lacking, and to never take a day for granted.

She attended the University of Kentucky, along with her high school sweetheart, and eventual husband and business partner, Dr. Chuck Verderber, who was a Division1 basketball player. Together, they have turned their wonder at the world, and comfort with risk, into a lifetime of making counter-intuitive choices that brought them challenges, lessons, and countless blessings.

Over the past thirty years they have built a unique dental practice in Northern Vermont with a focus on keeping the humanity in healthcare. Dr. Lynda's passion as a healthcare provider comes from her deep love for people, sharing laughter, tears, and hugs with patients who feel like family. This deep feeling of connectedness inspired yet another mission: to show others how they can usher in a new era for themselves and the world, one where discovery replaces division and collaboration will be the new social contract over contempt and confrontation.

In 2014, inspired by a young patient's comments, she created what we all wished existed on the internet: a place with no politics or ads where we can all feel confident about the future, Ever Widening Circles!

Ever Widening Circles is a media company on a mission to change the negative dialogue about our times. The content there points to insights, innovations, and good news that proves it's still an amazing world!

Since Ever Widening Circles (EWC) was founded, Dr. Lynda and her team have published over a thousand articles, curating the web for content that shows that progress and wonder are all around us. Every week she talks to ingenious and courageous thought leaders from around the world, and now, she's sharing their insights and stories with all of us!

Learning from the wonder and diversity of the human condition has deeply shaped her and the passions that fuel Ever Widening Circles. Her journey as a thought leader seems the logical outcome of life spent experiencing a deep connection with others and appreciating their ingenuity, wisdom and dreams.

*"I look for beauty instead of truth, and I stumble upon truth a lot more often."*

*– Dr. Lynda M. Ulrich*

# ENDNOTES

## Chapter One

[1] Jankowski, N. "Spread the Word: Butter Has an Epic Backstory." NPR. 24 Feb. 2017. https://www.npr.org/sections/thesalt/2017/02/24/515422661/spread-the-word-butter-has-an-epic-backstory. Accessed 5 May. 2020.

## Chapter Two

[2] History.com Editors. "Underground Railroad." HISTORY. 8 Feb. 2019. https://www.history.com/topics/black-history/underground-railroad. Accessed 13 May. 2020.

[3] Sifferlin, A. "ALS Ice Bucket Challenge: How it Started." Time. 18 Aug. 2014. https://time.com/3136507/als-ice-bucket-challenge-started/. Accessed 13 May. 2020.

[4] Ulrich, L. "#ConspiracyofGoodness: A Movement Changing our Future ...." 22 Apr. 2019. https://everwideningcircles.com/2019/04/22/conspiracyofgoodness-movement-changing-the-future/. Accessed 13 May. 2020.

[5] Grimes, W. "The Pride and Terror of Those Who Fought to the Death." The New York Times. 9 Dec. 2005. https://www.nytimes.com/2005/12/09/books/the-pride-and-terror-of-those-who-fought-to-the-death.html. Accessed 27 Mar. 2020.

## Chapter Three

[6] Ulrich, L. "Micro-Preemie Turns 21: A Success Story for Everyone!" EWC. 22 Jul. 2018. https://everwideningcircles.com/2018/07/22/micro-premie-success-story/. Accessed 14 May. 2020.

## Chapter Four

[7] "Learn About Brother David Steindl-Rast." Gratefulness.org. https://gratefulness.org/brother-david/about-brother-david/. Accessed 20 Apr. 2020.

[8] "EWCed - Ever Widening Circles." https://ed.everwideningcircles.com/. Accessed 20 Apr. 2020.

## Chapter Five

[9] "Web Growth Summary - MIT." https://www.mit.edu/people/mkgray/net/web-growth-summary.html. Accessed 31 Mar. 2020.

[10] "Total number of Websites." Internet Live Stats. https://www.internetlivestats.com/total-number-of-websites/. Accessed 31 Mar. 2020.

[11] OurWorldinData.org

[12] History.com Editors. "Child Labor - Laws, Definition & Industrial Revolution." History. 17 Apr. 2020, https://www.history.com/topics/industrial-revolution/child-labor. Accessed 1 May. 2020.

## Chapter Six

[13] Troncale, J., M.D. "Your Lizard Brain | Psychology Today." 23 Apr. 2014, https://www.psychologytoday.com/us/blog/where-addiction-meets-your-brain/201404/your-lizard-brain. Accessed 20 Apr. 2020.

[14] Houser, K. "How many people do you need to change the world?" World Economic Forum." 12 Jun. 2018. https://www.weforum.org/agenda/2018/06/want-to-change-society-s-views-here-s-how-many-people-you-ll-need-on-your-side/. Accessed 27 Mar. 2020.

[15] Godin, S. "Calm Also Has a Coefficient." Seth's Blog https://seths.blog/2020/03/calm-also-has-a-coefficient/ Accessed 24 June 2020.

## Chapter Seven

[16] Price, C. "Putting Down Your Phone May Help You Live Longer."
The New York Times. 24 Apr. 2019,
https://www.nytimes.com/2019/04/24/well/mind/putting-down-your-phone-may-help-you-live-longer.html. Accessed 1 Apr. 2020.

## Chapter Eight

[17] Ulrich, L. "Skateboarding for Peace in Afghanistan." Ever
Widening Circles. 5 Feb. 2017.
https://everwideningcircles.com/2017/02/05/skateboarding-peace-in-afghanistan/. Accessed 26 Mar. 2020.

[18] Verderber, Andrew. "What if trash pick-up was annual?." Ever
Widening Circles. 24 Apr. 2016.
https://everwideningcircles.com/2016/04/24/reducing-garbage-annually/. Accessed 27 Mar. 2020.

[19] "About Bea." Zero Waste Home.
https://zerowastehome.com/about/bea/. Accessed 30 Mar. 2020.

[20] "ABOUT LAUREN." Trash is for Tossers.
http://trashisfortossers.com/about-lauren/. Accessed 30 Mar. 2020.

## Chapter Nine

[21] "Celebrate What's Right." https://celebratewhatsright.com/. Accessed 20 Apr. 2020.

[22] https://www.planetary.org/explore/projects/lightsail-solar-sailing/

[23] Stirone, S. "LightSail 2 Unfurls, Next Step Toward Space Travel by
Solar Sail." 23 Jul. 2019.
https://www.nytimes.com/2019/07/23/science/lightsail-solar-sail.html. Accessed 20 Apr. 2020.

[24] "The Planetary Society: Home." https://www.planetary.org/. Accessed 21 Apr. 2020.

[25] "Bill Nye." https://www.billnye.com/. Accessed 21 Apr. 2020.

## Chapter Ten

[26] "Conversations Worth Having: Home." https://conversationsworthhaving.today/. Accessed 10 Apr. 2020.

[27] Carlowicz, M. "New Simulation Shows Consequences of a World without Earth's Natural Sunscreen." 18 Mar. 2009. https://www.nasa.gov/topics/earth/features/world_avoided.html. Accessed 6 Apr. 2020.

[28] Flight, C. "Smallpox: Eradicating the Scourge." BBC. 17 Feb. 2011. https://www.bbc.co.uk/history/british/empire_seapower/smallpox_01.shtml. Accessed 6 Apr. 2020.

[29] Kweifio-Okai, C. "Where did the Indian Ocean tsunami aid money go?" The Guardian. 25 Dec. 2014. https://www.theguardian.com/global-development/2014/dec/25/where-did-indian-ocean-tsunami-aid-money-go. Accessed 6 Apr. 2020.

[30] Dhillon, A. "'More deadly than terrorism': potholes responsible for killing 10 people a day in India." 24 Jul. 2018. https://www.theguardian.com/world/2018/jul/25/more-deadly-than-terrorism-potholes-responsible-for-killing-10-people-a-day-in-india. Accessed 18 Mar. 2020.

[31] Burns, S. "Why Would One Man Fill 600 Potholes?" Ever Widening Circles. 21 Jun. 2019. https://everwideningcircles.com/2019/06/21/potholes/. Accessed 18 Mar. 2020.

[32] Hartman, S. "Man who naps with cats helped raise $100,000 for pet sanctuary." CBS Evening News. https://www.cbsnews.com/news/terry-lauerman-man-who-naps-with-cats-helped-raise-thousands-for-pet-sanctuary/. Accessed 27 Mar. 2020.

[33] "Safe Haven Pet Sanctuary | Green Bay, Wisconsin." https://www.safehavenpet.org/. Accessed 27 Mar. 2020.

[34] Burns, S. "Why is this Busker Giving All of His Money Away?" Ever Widening Circles. 10 Apr. 2020.

https://everwideningcircles.com/2020/04/10/hopeful-cases-street-performer-will-boyajian/. Accessed 13 Apr. 2020.

35 "Hopeful Cases." https://www.hopefulcases.org/. Accessed 14 May 2020.

## Chapter Eleven

36 CBS News. "Consumers to Companies: You Better Stand for Something." https://www.cbsnews.com/news/edelman-earned-brand-study-2018-consumers-want-companies-to-stand-for-something/. Retrieved on June 13,2020

37 Glassdoor Team. "New Survey: Company mission and culture matter more than compensation." https://www.glassdoor.com/employers/blog/mission-culture-survey/. Retrieved on June 13, 2020.

38 Tonello, M. "The Business Case for Corporate Social Responsibility." Harvard Law School Forum on Corporate Governance. 26 Jun. 2011. https://corpgov.law.harvard.edu/2011/06/26/the-business-case-for-corporate-social-responsibility/. Accessed 14 May. 2020.

39 McPherson, S. "Corporate Responsibility: What to Expect In 2019." Forbes. 14 Jan. 2019. https://www.forbes.com/sites/susanmcpherson/2019/01/14/corporate-responsibility-what-to-expect-in-2019/. Accessed 14 May. 2020.

40 "LEGO Sustainable packaging 2025." LEGO.com. 21 Apr. 2018. https://www.lego.com/en-us/aboutus/news/2018/april/lego-sustainable-packaging-2025/. Accessed 18 Mar. 2020.

41 "The UPS Foundation Supports Ghana's Launch of the World's Largest Vaccine Drone Delivery Network." UPS.com. 24 Apr. 2019. https://pressroom.ups.com/pressroom/ContentDetailsViewer.page?ConceptType=PressReleases&id=1556027218757-179. Accessed 18 Mar. 2020.

42 "The Sato Project - Marc Jacobs."
https://www.marcjacobs.com/north-america/sato-project.html. Accessed 18 Mar. 2020.

43 Ulrich, Lynda M. "The Gratitude Economy is Changing Business for the Better!" 17 Oct. 2019.
https://everwideningcircles.com/2019/10/17/csr-corporate-social-responsibility-gratitude-economy/. Accessed 27 Mar. 2020.

44 "Five North Chocolate." https://www.fivenorthchocolate.com/. Accessed 14 May. 2020.

45 Kateman, B. "Buying Chocolate for Halloween? The Production Of Cocoa is Scarier Than You Think." 22 Oct. 2019.
https://www.forbes.com/sites/briankateman/2019/10/22/buying-chocolate-for-halloween-the-production-of-cocoa-is-scarier-than-you-think/. Accessed 14 May. 2020.

46 "GroFive Expandals - The ONLY shoes that GROW with your ...." https://grofive.com/. Accessed 14 May. 2020.

47 "The Shoe That Grows - Because International."
https://becauseinternational.org/the-shoe-that-grows. Accessed 14 May. 2020.

48 "2019 #ConspiracyofGoodness Holiday Gift Guide! | Ever Widening Circles." 26 Nov. 2019,
https://everwideningcircles.com/2019/11/26/2019-conspiracy-of-goodness-holiday-gift-guide/. Accessed 14 May. 2020.

49 "Bellcate School Dog Treat Business - Bellcate School."
https://bellcate.com/bellcate-dog-treat-company/. Accessed 14 May. 2020.

50 "About - Mother Trucker Yoga - No-mat yoga for truckers."
https://mothertruckeryoga.com/about/. Accessed 27 Mar. 2020.

51 "Buy a Pair, Give a Pair | Warby Parker."
https://www.warbyparker.com/buy-a-pair-give-a-pair. Accessed 27 Mar. 2020.

52 "Your Impact." TOMS.com." https://www.toms.com/impact. Accessed 27 Mar. 2020.

53 "Sock Donations - Giving Back – Bombas." https://bombas.com/pages/giving-back. Accessed 27 Mar. 2020.

54 "Total number of Websites." Internet Live Stats. https://www.internetlivestats.com/total-number-of-websites/. Accessed 13 Apr. 2020.

## Chapter Twelve

55 Ulrich-Verderber, L. "Saving the Rainforest with Old Cell Phones." Ever Widening Circles. 4 Apr. 2016. https://everwideningcircles.com/2016/04/04/saving-the-rainforest-with-old-cellphones/. Accessed 4 Apr. 2020.

56 Ulrich, L. "Old Cellphones: The Key to Stopping Climate Change." Ever Widening Circles." 20 May. 2019. https://everwideningcircles.com/2019/05/20/rainforest-connection-old-cellphones/. Accessed 4 Apr. 2020.

57 Ibid. Accessed 16 Mar. 2020.

58 Moss, David and Scheer, R. "Deforestation and Its Devastating Effect on Global Warming." Scientific America. November 13, 2012. https://www.scientificamerican.com/article/deforestation-and-global-warming/. Accessed on 16 June 2020.

59 Kennedy, J. "How AI and old phones can help to save the rainforests." Silicon Republic. 21 Feb. 2019. https://www.siliconrepublic.com/machines/rainforests-mobile-phones-ai-rainforest-connection-google. Accessed 16 Mar. 2020.

60 Shchetko, N. "Chainsaws, Gunshots and Coughs: Our Smartphones Are Listening." Wall Street Journal. 3 Jul. 2014, https://blogs.wsj.com/digits/2014/07/03/chainsaws-gunshots-and-coughs-our-smartphones-are-listening/. Accessed 27 Mar. 2020.

## Chapter Thirteen

[61] Gibbs, D.; Harris, N. and Seymour, Francis. "By the Numbers: The Value of Tropical Forests in the Climate Change Equation." World Resources Institute. 4 Oct. 2018, https://www.wri.org/blog/2018/10/numbers-value-tropical-forests-climate-change-equation. Accessed 16 Mar. 2020.

[62] Burns, Sam. "Red Rose Tattoo." Ever Widening Circles. 5 Mar. 2020. https://everwideningcircles.com/2020/03/05/red-rose-tattoo-billy-white/. Accessed 21 Apr. 2020.

[63] Burns, S. "Can You Fit a 2-Acre Garden in a Shipping Container." Ever Widening Circles. 4 Feb. 2020. https://everwideningcircles.com/2020/02/04/square-roots-urban-farming-shipping-containers/. Accessed 21 Apr. 2020.

[64] Ulrich-Verderber, L. "How Seizure Response Dogs are Changing People's Lives." Ever Widening Circles. 9 Jun. 2019. https://everwideningcircles.com/2019/06/09/seizure-response-dogs/. Accessed 21 Apr. 2020.

[65] Burns, Sam. "Restoring Sight to the Blind with a $3 Innovation. https://everwideningcircles.com/2020/06/01/cataracts-innovation-healthcare-nepal/?swcfpc=1. Accessed June 13,2020.

[66] Ulrich, L. "Single Mothers are Saving Africa's Endangered Wildlife." Ever Widening Circles. 3 Nov. 2018. https://everwideningcircles.com/2018/11/03/single-moms-train-as-wildlife-rangers/. Accessed 13 May. 2020.

[67] Berlinger, J. "World's last male northern white rhino dies." CNN.com. 20 Mar. 2018. https://www.cnn.com/2018/03/20/africa/last-male-white-rhino-dies-intl/index.html. Accessed 26 Mar. 2020.

[68] Nuwer, R. "'Brave Ones': The women saving Africa's wildlife." BBC. 27 Sep. 2018. https://www.bbc.com/future/article/20180926-akashinga-all-women-rangers-in-africa-fighting-poaching. Accessed 26 Mar. 2020.

[69] Barber, J. "Africa's new elite force: women gunning for poachers and fighting for a better life." The Guardian. 16 Dec. 2017. https://www.theguardian.com/environment/2017/dec/17/poaching-wildlife-africa-conservation-women-barbee-zimbabwe-elephant-rhino. Accessed 27 Mar. 2020.

[70] Mander, Damien. (May 2013). "Modern Warrior." Retrieved from https://www.youtube.com/watch?v=9FCsyK4aRXQ

[71] Ibid. Accessed 13 Apr. 2020.

## Chapter Fourteen

[72]Ulrich, Lynda M. "Principal Wayman's Recipe for Changing Schools and Lives." https://everwideningcircles.com/2019/08/26/principal-wayman-currently-trending/?swcfpc=1

[73] Ulrich-Verderber, L. "Sailing Through Space on the Power of the Sun." Ever Widening Circles. 22 Aug. 2019. https://everwideningcircles.com/2019/08/22/lightsail-2-the-planetary-society-bill-nye/. Accessed 14 May. 2020.

[74] Ulrich-Verderber, L. "What Do Astronauts Dream About?" Ever Widening Circles." 15 Sep. 2016. https://everwideningcircles.com/2016/09/15/what-an-astronaut-dreams/. Accessed 30 Mar. 2020.

[75] Ulrich, L. "Living Beyond Expectations: Daniel Kish." Ever Widening Circles." 29 Oct. 2017. https://everwideningcircles.com/2017/10/29/daniel-kish-life-beyond-expectations/. Accessed 30 Mar. 2020.

[76] Ulrich-Verderber, L. "Welcome to the Worldwide Web, Meet the Internet of Fungus!" Ever Widening Circles. 9 Feb. 2017, https://everwideningcircles.com/2017/02/09/the-internet-of-fungus/. Accessed 30 Mar. 2020.

[77] Burns, S. "You Should Really Thank the Fruit Flies." Ever Widening Circles. 23 Jan. 2018. https://everwideningcircles.com/2018/01/23/ode-to-fruit-flies/. Accessed 30 Mar. 2020.

[78] "What Makes Your Dogs Sense of Smell So Great? | EWC." 9 Jul. 2019, https://everwideningcircles.com/2019/07/09/dogs-sense-of-smell/. Accessed 6 Apr. 2020.

[79] Burns, S. "A New Look at Life from the World's First Cyborg!" Ever Widening Circles. 8 Apr. 2020. https://everwideningcircles.com/2020/04/08/neil-harbisson-cyborg-hearing-colors/. Accessed 14 May. 2020.

[80] Ulrich, L. "Discover the Man Who Sees Only with Sound! He's Redefining What's "Impossible!" Ever Widening Circles. 31 Jul. 2019, https://everwideningcircles.com/2019/07/31/daniel-kish-blind-seeing-with-sound/. Accessed 27 Mar. 2020.

[81] Ibid. Accessed 30 Mar. 2020.

**Chapter Fifteen**

[82] Ulrich, L. "What if We Celebrated What's Right in the World?" Ever Widening Circles. 7 Jul. 2019, https://everwideningcircles.com/2019/07/07/the-potential-in-celebrating-whats-right-with-the-world/. Accessed 6 Apr. 2020.

[83] "Conversations Worth Having: Home." https://conversationsworthhaving.today/. Accessed 10 Apr. 2020.